PORK, BEEF, CHICKEN AND RIBS

PORK, BEEF, CHICKEN AND RIBS

CHEWING ON
RELIGIOUS TRUTHS

HAROLD OWEN GREGG

TATE PUBLISHING
AND ENTERPRISES, LLC

Pork, Beef, Chicken and Ribs
Copyright © 2014 by Harold Owen Gregg. All rights reserved.

No part of this publication may be reproduced, stored in a retrieval system or transmitted in any way by any means, electronic, mechanical, photocopy, recording or otherwise without the prior permission of the author except as provided by USA copyright law.

Scripture quotations taken from the New American Standard Bible®, Copyright © 1960, 1962, 1963, 1968, 1971, 1972, 1973, 1975, 1977, 1995 by The Lockman Foundation. Used by permission.

The opinions expressed by the author are not necessarily those of Tate Publishing, LLC.

Published by Tate Publishing & Enterprises, LLC
127 E. Trade Center Terrace | Mustang, Oklahoma 73064 USA
1.888.361.9473 | www.tatepublishing.com

Tate Publishing is committed to excellence in the publishing industry. The company reflects the philosophy established by the founders, based on Psalm 68:11,
"The Lord gave the word and great was the company of those who published it."

Book design copyright © 2014 by Tate Publishing, LLC. All rights reserved.
Cover design by Gian philipp Rufin
Interior design by Jomar Ouano

Published in the United States of America
ISBN: 978-1-63063-815-3
1. Religion / Christian Theology / General
2. Religion / Islam / Koran & Sacred Writings
14.04.28

The Koran which I quote is the Ballantine Books Edition of April 1993, and is based on the original English translation by J. M. Rodwell, and bears the identification of ISBN 0-8041-1125-1.

CONTENTS

Preface 9
Introduction 13

The Ransom Agreement 29
The Apostle Paul 43
The Spiritual Realm 53

The Koran 61
   Introduction 61
   The Story of Civilization 64
   Teachings from the Koran 74
   Opposing Christian and Islamic Theology 89
   Jesus Described in the Koran 99
   Retaliation 105
   The Noah Stories 110
   Divorce in the Koran 118
   Other Teachings 119
   Summary 122

The Christian Bible 129
   Introduction 129
   Interpretation of the Bible 131
   Accuracy of the Bible 134
   Teachings from the Bible 141
   Prophesy in the Bible 145
   The New Covenant 149
   Summary of the Old Testament 157
   The New Testament 165
   The Requirements for Salvation 170
   Promises from God 177
   The Trinity 181
   The Holy Spirit 185
   Joy the Proof of our Salvation 189

The Apostle Paul 193
Islam, the Apostasy of Christianity 195
Brainwashing 203
The Conflicting Theologies 209
The Gathering of God's People 215
Where Do We Go from Here 231

PREFACE

We live in a world that is real and beautiful and in a universe that is astounding with its beauty and its complexity, and we accept that it is real because we can touch it and compute a flight path to the moon and the planets. We are told that there is a spiritual world, which we will enter into when we die, and that we will live there for eternity.

There are many people who find this idea rather "far-fetched" and question whether that spiritual realm exists at all, and then there are those of us who have been touched by the spiritual realm and know that it is there. The most important decision that anyone can make is to delve into a study of the spiritual realm; and if that person is very lucky, he or she will prove to themselves that the spiritual realm does exist and then live their lives here on this earth in a way which insures their entry into it.

Our religion is centered upon the spiritual realm. Proof that the spiritual realm exists is varied, valid, and can be determined by anyone willing to attempt to become familiar with it. First you must have a reverence for God whom you are seeking to know, and you must come with truthfulness.

The Lord spoke to Moses, "By those who come near Me I will be treated as holy" (Lev. 10:3, NASB). The apostle Paul makes this important observation:

> While we look not at the things which are seen, but at the things which are not seen; for the things which are seen are temporal, but the things which are not seen are eternal.
>
> 2 Corinthians 4:18 (NASB)

In a dream I found myself in heaven, and I questioned what I should do. The answer was for me to sing praise to God. As I raised my voice to sing, I was surprised by the grand sound of it, and a multitude of other voices joined with mine in this praise to God, and the sound was magnificent. As the song of praise ended, the most wonderful feeling enveloped my whole being, and I know that this is how the spirit feels in heaven when the love of God surrounds you.

When God wraps you in his love, every fiber in your body reacts with joy. Even though I was dreaming, the feeling was real, and I recognized at the time that the feeling was coming from God. I wanted to remain in that state forever, but I could not.

As I awakened and realized that I was still alive, I was filled with remorse, sat on the side of my bed, and cried profusely until my mouth was dry from so many tears. God made me to understand that I must make a choice between the life I had been living, and a life pleasing to him. I was in danger of losing the opportunity to ever experience that heavenly feeling again.

I was fearful that I had reached the limits of God's patience and in danger of being separated from him forever. That feeling of God's all-encompassing love caused me to change my life around and drove me to seek him to this day. That drive has not diminished with time; even though worldly concerns sometimes interfere. That encounter motivated me to learn all that I could about God because I desperately wanted to be on the right path, which he requires, and because I had been shown what it was like to be in heaven.

In heaven, you are completely encased in God's love, and it is an indescribable pleasure. Psalm 16, verse 11 states that in God's right hand there are pleasures forever, and in Isaiah 65:17, we learn that things of this earth will not be remembered or come to mind. There is no pleasure on this earth that compares with the pleasure of being in heaven.

There are important prophesies that I find interconnected to reveal the plans that God has made for this universe. First, when he called me to follow his plan for salvation, he gave me the feeling of being wrapped in his love which I perceive is what it is like to be in heaven. Then as I began to seriously study in order to make myself approved by God, I was afforded an understanding of the scriptures that made me recognize his plan. Now, it is necessary for me to write this treatise.

During the exodus, God began to reveal his plan through Moses. Then through Prophet Zechariah he reveals that only a third of humanity will become his people, and that he will test them in their dedication to him. Amos also revealed that there would be a time that God's word would not be available to the people, and calls that, "a famine for the word of God."

Through Prophets Isaiah and Jeremiah, God expands on his plan for a new covenant, and he reveals that this new covenant will be for the whole world. It will result in salvation for his people, and it will be ushered in by a descendant of David. Through most of the prophets, other changes to occur because of his new covenant are revealed, which are centered on changes to take place in the relationship between the world we know and the spiritual world.

The forecast was for an end to the prophets, fortune-tellers, diviners, and soothsayers, and it would denote a definite increase in separation between the physical world and the spiritual. Then in an unusual move, God tells of paying a ransom in order to secure the provisions of his new covenant, and calls himself "Redeemer" by virtue of that transaction. Prophesy then slows until the Apostles of the one sent to usher in the new covenant begin to reveal what will occur at a later time. The Apostle Paul makes the most astounding of these revelations by telling of the apostasy that must occur before the end-time, and he warns of the force perpetrating the apostasy. Secular history reveals the force that renounces God's plan for our salvation is the religion of Islam. The purpose of this treatise is to inform God's people of that force.

I began to study Islam in 2002, which was shortly before the attack by al Qaeda. I have read through the Koran about ten times and studied portions of it in detail. My study includes history of religion from paganism to the Reformation. I have come to know God's plan and how this plan has progressed throughout time.

I want to tell others what I have learned. The conclusions, which I have reached is my interpretation from all the inputs from the Bible, The Koran, the history of Christianity, and secular history. There will be many theologians that will disagree with my interpretation, and that is to be expected; however, I am convinced of its correctness.

INTRODUCTION

There is a power in this world that prescribes good, and another power that prescribes evil. These two forces appear to coexist under strict rules of engagement. The creator of all of this is God, the force for good, who created the heavens and the earth and all that is contained there-in; and this includes the power for evil, who is known by the names: Lucifer, Satan, the devil, the deceiver, the serpent, the great dragon, the accuser, and perhaps other names we are not apprised of.

It is the desire of the evil force to destroy that which was created. Satan, the evil force, can only exercise power that was allowed him by the Creator—God, the power for good. God actively seeks the devotion of his creation, and has given his creation the authority to choose whether to grant him reverence. I assume that spiritual beings created by God have the same authority because we are shown where Lucifer, the angelic name for Satan, rebelled against God seeking his own dominion. We refer to this authority to make our own decisions as "free will," for we are free to choose good or to choose evil. The evil one is also known as the deceiver; and he will misdirect people whenever possible, into choosing what is evil. Deception is not a characteristic of the true God, nor is it possible for him to lie.

There is a promise from God that he does nothing in secret. The earliest of the prophetic books quoted in the Bible is Amos. Amos tells us that God does nothing in secret, and that a prophet has no choice but to pass along the word of God that he receives. I interpret this passage as a promise from God that the average person can understand what the Bible teaches without special abilities or special formula.

> Surely the Lord God does nothing unless he reveals his secret counsel to his servants the prophets. A lion has roared! Who will not fear? The Lord God has spoken! Who can but prophesy?
>
> Amos 3:7–8 (NASB)

The use of the word "surely" makes this a very profound statement because it means without doubt. I have found this promise to be true. I have been led through the last half of my life into the knowledge of God and his plan for *mankind*. The Lord God has spoken, and those who will hear will be glorious. If you have ears to hear, please listen, because this plan is from God and there is no input from any other source.

We learn from Amos many of the characteristics of God, and especially his love for justice, and the idea that justice will be the plumb line which will be used to judge a man or a nation. We learn of the end of the nation Israel at Amos 8:1–10 where they are likened to a bowl of summer fruit, which has become overripe and not appealing to him. The entire book of Amos seems to be a complaint from God on the lack of proper response from the Hebrew people for their God. Only a few verses from the entire book of Amos are applicable to us today. We can learn many things from Amos and his announcements establish him as a prophet of God. When I call just a few verses significant for us, it is not to decrease the importance of the remainder of the book. If we take away all the writing directed toward the

Hebrew people for that period, there are only a few verses that remain, and that is the prophesy of a famine for the word of God, and the prophesy of a new Israel; so out of the book of Amos, only a few verses need to be discussed here.

Note that the prophesy for the "famine" is definitely for future times, and it was a provision of the ransom agreement.

> Behold, days are coming, declares the Lord God, "When I will send a famine on the land, Not a famine for bread or a thirst for water, But rather for hearing the words of the Lord. "People will stagger from sea to sea And from the north even to the east; They will go to and fro to seek the word of the Lord, But they will not find it.
>
> Amos 8:11–12 (NASB)

This famine for the word of God is never mentioned again in the Bible, so in order to recognize such a famine, we must rely on secular history and we find the fulfillment of this famine prophesy in the history of Christianity. Such a famine would not be possible today with all the memory available within the computer industry; but there was a time that began in AD 210, when Bishop Ciprian restricted access of the scripture to the clergy, and fulfilled this prophesy. This famine was further aggravated following Jerome's translation of the Bible into Latin (The Vulgate), when Damasus (Bishop of Rome AD 366–384) proclaimed that all scriptures must be read in Latin. Within about 120 years after the death of the apostle John, that grand story of salvation was not accessible to the common man, and was then hidden from the entire world with the exception of the clergy. This famine for the Word of God permitted the unencumbered rise of the religion of Islam. The famine ended with the Reformation and the invention of the printing press and then publication of the first New Testament printed in Greek in 1514.

About the same time the Reformation gained momentum and Christianity exploded into the new world, America. The new Israel prophesy by Amos could be interpreted to be for this same land, America. The time line for the end of the famine for the word of God corresponds with the obvious time line for the end of the ransom agreement provision that God not interfere within that area of the world given in ransom to Satan.

> Also I will restore the captivity of my people Israel, and they will rebuild the ruined cities and live in them; they will also plant vineyards and drink their wine, and make gardens and eat their fruit. "I will also plant them on their land, And they will not again be rooted out from their land Which I have given them," says the Lord your God.
>
> Amos 9:14–15 (NASB)

In the beginning, God promised to inform us of the future, and he has kept that promise. Every important occurrence was foretold by God's servants, the *prophets*. The most important of these was the ratification of a new covenant, so it is important to know how that covenant came about and all its provisions. The new covenant was mentioned by God to Moses after God had spoken the Ten Commandments directly to the people assembled at Horeb. The words were so fearful to the people, that they asked Moses to speak to them what God spoke, but they did not want to hear directly from the mouth of God anymore for fear of death. God then said to Moses:

> They have spoken well; I will raise up a prophet from among their countrymen like you, and I will put my words in his mouth, and he shall speak to them all that I command him. It shall come about that whoever will not listen to my words which he shall speak in my name, I myself will require it of him.
>
> Deuteronomy 18:17–19 (NASB)

Then the promise of the new covenant is made.

> Behold, days are coming," declares the Lord, "when I will make a new covenant with the house of Israel and with the house of Judah, not like the covenant which I made with their fathers in the day I took them by the hand to bring them out of the land of Egypt, my covenant which they broke, although I was a husband to them," declares the Lord. "But this is the covenant which I will make with the house of Israel after those days," declares the Lord, "I will put my law within them and on their heart I will write it and I will be their God, and they shall be my people." "They will not teach again each man his neighbor and each man his brother, saying 'Know the Lord,' for they will all know me, from the lest of them to the greatest of them," declares the Lord, "for I will forgive their iniquity, and their sin I will remember no more.
>
> Jeremiah 31:31–34 (NASB)

Just two chapters later, God explains this promise to be inclusive of all the earth.

> Behold, days are coming," declares the Lord, "when I will fulfill the good word which I have spoken concerning the house of Israel and the house of Judah. In those days and at that time I will cause a righteous Branch of David to spring forth; and he shall execute justice and righteousness on the earth.
>
> Jeremiah 33: 14–15 (NASB)

Take note of these two things; justice and righteousness (simply what is right), because they are very important to God.

Jeremiah prophesied in Judah beginning about 626 BC until about 586 BC. It is important to note here that the covenant is a contract made by God, and it establishes what he will do in the lives of those affected by the covenant. Mankind has absolutely no authority to say what the covenant requires or what it provides. The new covenant is optional—it can be ignored, or rejected, or accepted.

The people, who take hold of the new covenant, are referred to in the Bible by the same name "Israel," as the people who were included in the old covenant. One must look to the period in order to know whether a passage of scripture is referring to the family of Abraham or the new Israel (those who take hold of the new covenant). This righteous Branch of David, who will execute justice and righteousness on earth, is called by other names by other prophets in the Bible—The Son of God, the Holy One of Israel, Redeemer, Savior, God's own right arm, the Christ, the Messiah, and some others. Prophesy was so explicit about the coming of the Savior that the people knew that he would be born in Bethlehem. There were others who claimed to be the Christ before Jesus. Two such persons are told about by Gamaliel, who was a respected teacher of the law. Peter and the Apostles were before the Senate Council in Jerusalem and Peter was speaking:

> The God of our fathers raised up Jesus, whom you had put to death by hanging him on a cross. He is the one whom God exalted to his right hand as a Prince and a Savior, to grant repentance to Israel, and forgiveness of sins. "And we are witnesses of these things; and so is the Holy Spirit, whom God has given to those who obey him." But when they heard this, they were cut to the quick and intended to kill them. But a Pharisee named Gamaliel, a teacher of the Law, respected by all the people, stood up in the Council and gave orders to put the men outside for a short time. And he said to them, "Men of Israel, take care what you propose to do with these men. "For some time ago Theudas rose up, claiming to be somebody, and a group of about four hundred men joined up with him. But he was killed, and all who followed him were dispersed and

came to nothing. "After this man, Judas of Galilee rose up in the days of the census and drew away some people after him; he too perished, and all those who followed him were scattered. "So in the present case, I say to you, stay away from these men and let them alone, for if this plan or action is of men, it will be overthrown; but if it is of God, you will not be able to overthrow them; or else you may even be found fighting against God." They took his advice; and after calling the apostles in, they flogged them and ordered them not to speak in the name of Jesus, and then released them. So they went on their way from the presence of the Council, rejoicing that they had been considered worthy to suffer shame for his name. And every day, in the temple and from house to house, they kept right on teaching and preaching Jesus as the Christ.

Acts 5:30–42 (NASB)

There comes a time in the Scriptures where the name "Israel" takes on a new and different meaning. This happens when God's new covenant is finalized, and his interest is toward the new Israel rather than the nation Israel. This new covenant is God's plan and it provides a sure salvation through faith in Jesus Christ. This is the Christian faith to which we subscribe. Paul says that through faith in Christ Jesus, we have all become sons of God, and if you belong to Christ, then you are Abraham's descendants, heirs according to the promise. Paul also explains that they are not all Israel, who are descended from Abraham, but we are Israel who believe God and have faith in Christ. Read what Paul wrote about faith:

> But the Scripture has shut up everyone under sin, so that the promise by faith in Jesus Christ might be given to those who believe. But before faith came, we were kept in custody under the law, being shut up to the faith which was later to be revealed. Therefore the Law has become our tutor to lead us to Christ, so that we may be justified by

faith. But now that faith has come, we are no longer under a tutor. For you are all sons of God through faith in Christ Jesus. For all of you who were baptized into Christ have clothed yourselves with Christ. There is neither Jew nor Greek, there is neither slave nor free man, there is neither male nor female; for you are all one in Christ Jesus. And if you belong to Christ, then you are Abraham's descendants, heirs according to promise.

Galatians 3:22–29 (NASB)

In Gal. 6:16, Paul refers to us as "the Israel of God." This change from ancestral Israel is evident at the end of Isaiah chapter 42, to a new Israel at the beginning of chapter 43. It is here that the ransom agreement is described, a trade-off that apparently ratified the new covenant throughout all of creation. Fortune-tellers, soothsayers, diviners, and prophets were to end with the implementation of the new covenant. This was the provision that decreased the power of the evil forces and increased the separation between the physical world and the spiritual world. People who possessed the ability to interact with the spiritual realm, often made their living from that talent, like the slave girl making money for her masters by fortune-telling in Acts 16. The Old Testament prophets, Micah and Zechariah, both tell of the end of evil spirits and prophets that will occur at a later time.

> It will come about in that day," declares the Lord of hosts, "that I will cut off the names of the idols from the land, and they will no longer be remembered; and I will also remove the prophets and the unclean spirit from the land.
>
> Zechariah 13:2 (NASB)

> I will cut off sorceries from your hand, And you will have fortune-tellers no more.
>
> Micah 5:12 (NASB)

The changes that occurred in the spiritual realm were much more drastic than those evident on earth because the Devil was cast out of heaven with all his angels; therefore, evil was eliminated from the spiritual world. Now heaven is prepared as a place of rest for our souls. Through Zechariah God told that two thirds of mankind will perish and one third will remain. He made a promise that he would refine the one third that remains and that they would be his people. This is the language that is used to describe the people who come to him by the new covenant and referred to as the new Israel.

> It will come about in all the land," declares the Lord, "that two parts in it will be cut off and perish; but the third will be left in it. And I will bring the third part through the fire, refine them as silver is refined, and test them as gold is tested. They will call on my name, and I will answer them; I will say, 'they are my people,' and they will say, 'The Lord is my God.'
>
> Zechariah 13:8–9 (NASB)

The metaphor of refining and testing gold and silver is used when the testing of God's people is the subject. Read this change now from Isaiah.

> Who gave Jacob up for spoil, and Israel to plunderers? Was it not the Lord, against whom we have sinned, and in whose ways they were not willing to walk, and whose laws they did not obey? So he poured out on him the heat of his anger and the fierceness of battle; and it set him aflame all around, yet he did not recognize it; and it burned him, but he paid no attention.
>
> Isaiah 42: 24–25 (NASB)

It was the ancestral Israel that God gave up for spoil. God had dealt with ancestral Israel since the days of Moses until this time that corresponds with Cyrus of Persia freeing them from bondage, about 539 BC. Israel had failed the testing by God so the metaphorical heat from the refining process burned them but they did not recognize it; therefore his rejection of them. Now read about the new Israel still from Isaiah.

> But now, thus says the Lord, your Creator, O Jacob, and he who formed you, O Israel, "Do no fear, for I have redeemed you; I have called you by name; you are mine! When you pass through the waters, I will be with you, and through the rivers, they will not overflow you. When you walk through the fire, you will not be scorched, nor will the flame burn you. For I am the Lord your God, the Holy One of Israel, Your Savior; I have given Egypt as your ransom, Cush and Seba in your place. Since you are precious in my sight, since you are honored and I love you, I will give other men in your place and other peoples in exchange for your life. Do not fear, for I am with you; I will bring your offspring from the east and gather you from the west. I will say to the north, 'give them up,' and to the south, 'do not hold them back.' Bring my sons from afar and my daughters from the ends of the earth, everyone who is called by my name, and whom I have created for my glory, whom I have formed, even whom I have made.
>
> Isaiah 43: 1–7 (NASB)

This passage demonstrates the extreme measures God has taken to insure the new covenant, and this ransom agreement is the act that ratified that covenant. It also demonstrates his great love for those who will come to him by way of this new covenant; even to call them, "precious in his sight." The apostle Paul coined the phrase "Israel of God" in Galatians 6:16 for those people who are of the household of faith, where he describes those being saved through Christ Jesus. Paul describes the new children of God throughout the book of Galatians, as well as in other of his writings. A passage, that accompanies the gathering together of the new Israel from whence they have been scattered, reads, "I will be their God, and they shall be my people." This passage usually accompanies any prophesy concerning the people of the new covenant, and is one way that makes it easy to determine whether the subject is ancestral Israel or the new Israel. The prophesy of gathering later generations known by God's name is made more significant because it is told in the same breath telling of the ransom.

There comes a time in the scriptural record when negotiations between God and Satan came to an end, and both agreed to the new covenant. There were many provisions included within this new covenant, and they were to have occurred in a certain order of time, which I call a timeline. The major occurrence was the coming of a Savior, the Messiah, Jesus Christ, through which salvation was to be offered to all people on the earth. The power of Satan was to decrease. The interaction between the spiritual world and the physical world was to change drastically, so that most interaction between them would come to an end.

For Satan to agree with all the provisions of this new covenant, he demanded to be worshipped as a god, and a geographical area of the world was selected by him where his lordship was to rule. Provisions were agreed upon which promoted Satan's lordship and a period of time was established, whereby God would not interfere with Satan's plan. I will attempt to show all the provisions included within this new covenant by scriptural reference or secular history.

The evil force in the universe, which we call Satan, is powerful; however, prior to the death of Jesus on the cross, he was much more powerful. We know from the book of Job that God permitted Satan to have power over all that Job had, but he could not take Job's life. We learned also that Satan roamed the earth and had access before God in heaven. We learn in Revelation 12:10 that the devil would point out our sins to God both day and night, which indicates a continual accusation. Distasteful? Yes. Yet God permitted him to do so. This indicates that Satan had some right to defy God with impunity, or at the least it indicates that he had a relationship with God that permitted access to God without restrictions. How can this relationship be explained correctly? We must learn more about the powers of Satan.

There are scriptural references which allude to the powers wielded by the forces of evil sufficient to recognize that they held greater power prior to the start of the new covenant. The most explicit reference is from 1 Samuel 28:15, and the story needs to be read from verse 7:

> Then Saul said to his servants, "Seek for me a woman who is a medium, that I may go to her and inquire of her." And his servants said to him, "Behold, there is a woman who is a medium at Endor." Then Saul disguised himself by putting on other clothes, and went, he and two men with him, and they came to the woman by night; and he said, "Conjure up for me, please, and bring up for me whom I shall name to you." But the woman said to him, "Behold, you know what Saul has done, how he has cut off those who are mediums and spiritists from the land. Why are you then laying a snare for my life to bring about my death?" Saul vowed to her by the Lord, saying, "As the Lord lives, no punishment shall come upon you for this thing." Then the woman said, "Whom shall I bring up for you?" And he said, "Bring up Samuel for me." When the woman saw Samuel, she cried out with a loud voice; and the woman spoke to Saul, saying, "Why have you deceived me? For you are Saul." The king said to her, "Do not be afraid; but what do you see?" And the woman said to Saul, "I see a divine being coming up out of the earth." He said to her, "What is his form?" And she said, "An old man is coming up, and he is wrapped with a robe." And Saul knew that it was Samuel, and he bowed with his face to the ground and

did homage. Then Samuel said to Saul, "Why have you disturbed me by bringing me up?

1 Samuel 28:7–15 (NASB)

We know that Samuel was brought up against his will by what he said to Saul. Also evident is the power of the medium to call up any spirit from the dead. Also interesting is the order given by Saul to his servants; were all mediums women? It may be that males possessing these powers were called "diviners", as was Balaam son of Beor, who was a well-known diviner during the time of Moses, and his exploits are told about in Numbers chapters 22 and 23. One provision of the new covenant was a greater separation between the spiritual and the physical worlds, for spiritist and prophets were to cease. The fact that the forces of evil resisted the changes necessary to implement the new covenant become evident when the ransom paid to ratify it is described by Isaiah. Read again the ransom provisions.

> For I am the Lord your God, The Holy One of Israel, your Savior; I have given Egypt as your ransom, Cush and Seba in your place. Since you are precious in my sight, since you are honored and I love you, I will give other men in your place and other peoples in exchange for your life.
>
> Isaiah 43:3–4 (NASB)

In this passage, God tells of giving a part of the world to another, as a ransom in order to protect those he calls, "precious in my sight." God does not say to whom he paid the ransom, but Satan is the only other power with which God would be making such an arrangement. Apparently this arrangement ratified the new covenant. When the implementation of the new covenant was assured, God says that he has redeemed the new Israel or those precious in his sight. Satan apparently had the authority to demand the ransom, and because of this transaction, he then had a contractual obligation to accept all the other provisions of the new covenant. It becomes obvious in the follow on scripture that God is well pleased with the ransom agreement. When this ransom agreement was made, the area of the world ceded to Satan was most of the known developed world and when Satan was tempting Jesus, he showed him all the kingdoms of the world. Then he said to Jesus, "I will give you all this domain and its glory; for it has been handed over to me, and I give it to whomever I wish. Therefore, if you worship before me, it shall all be Yours" (Luke 4:5–7 NASB).

Contemplate how such an agreement would have been negotiated between God and Satan. God is all knowing, all powerful, and present in all space and time; while Satan does not have any of these powers; nor can God tell a lie or deceive. Satan would be at a disadvantage in any negotiations; therefore, the provisions of such an agreement must originate with Satan, because God cannot be unfair.

I believe that Satan gambled his place in heaven in order to receive power over a part of the earth, and he thought he could defeat God's plan. Satan had to think that he could prevail over a human son of God and cause him to sin. Throughout the recorded history in the Bible, Satan had succeeded in thwarting God's desires; so with such success, it is understandable that he would think that he could overcome a fully human Son of God. Understand that the new covenant must include all of creation, both heaven and earth, which means that we must consider the spiritual realm. All of heaven, the spiritual realm, had to know all the details of the new covenant and be prepared to enforce all of the provisions demanded by it. The ransom agreement was the pivotal point around which the new covenant was ratified. Isaiah does not say that this ransom agreement had a time limit. My summation that there was, is based upon the fact that it would be unlike God for no time limit to be specified. If no time limit existed then Satan would forever control a portion of God's creation, and that concept does not fall within reason. In other passages of scripture that may relate to this timeframe a period of time described by "a time and times and half a time" (Daniel 7:25, and Revelation 12:14). Read what happened when Satan lost his gamble.

> And there was war in heaven, Michael and his angels waging war with the dragon. The dragon and his angels waged war, and they were not strong enough, and there was no longer a place found for them in heaven. And the great dragon was thrown down, the serpent of old called the devil and Satan, who deceives the whole world; he was thrown down to the earth, and his angels were thrown down with him. Then I heard a loud voice in heaven, saying, "Now the salvation, and the power, and the kingdom of our God and the authority of his Christ have come, for the accuser of our brethren has been thrown down, he who accuses them before our God day and night. "And they overcame him because of the blood of the Lamb and because of the word of their testimony, and they did not love their life even when faced with death. "For this reason, rejoice, O heavens and you who dwell in them. Woe to the earth and the sea, because the devil has come down to you, having great wrath, knowing that he has only a short time.
>
> Revelation 12:7–12 (NASB)

In this passage the devil, the dragon, the serpent of old, and Satan are identified as the same person, and we learn that he is no longer allowed to dwell in heaven where he was accuser of those brethren as he did with Job. Notice that the deciding factor in this struggle between Michael and the devil was the blood of the Lamb that was slain, the blood of the Messiah, Jesus Christ. This bolsters the idea that the devil was cast down at the time of the death of Jesus who was faithful unto death on the cross. After hearing the report from the seventy that were sent out in pairs (Luke 10:1–18): upon the report that, "Lord, even the demons are subject to us in your name." Jesus said to them, "I was watching Satan fall from heaven like lightning. Psalm 22 appears to be a forecast of Jesus suffering on the cross. If we interpret this scripture in that way, it appears that throughout his suffering, he is respectful of the Father, and therefore without sin. I also believe that the provision to send the Holy Spirit to comfort the Christian believer was the provision most disliked by Satan because of the time which the Holy Spirit was given, and because of the statement by Jesus, made before his crucifixion that "if" he was raised up, He would send the Holy Spirit (John 16:7). It is the power of the Holy Spirit that provides a Christian with the power to resist Satan. Satan was evicted from heaven because of the blood of the lamb. The lamb of God, Jesus Christ. Satan lost his gamble when Jesus died on the cross free of sin. I suspect that the outcome would have been very different if Jesus had questioned God's actions. John 12:31 supports the casting out. That important story where Jesus tells of Satan being cast out of heaven should be read from verse twenty to the end of chapter twelve. The passage is too lengthy to be quoted here.

THE RANSOM AGREEMENT

A ransom agreement (Isaiah 43:1–7) ratified the new covenant and gave to Satan a part of the world—to do with as he pleased for a time, and, in return, Satan agreed to all the provisions of God's new covenant with the universe. God was well pleased with this trade-off and calls himself the "Redeemer," by virtue of it. God has done a great thing and he wants to be recognized for it.

> I have wiped out your transgressions like a thick cloud and your sins like a heavy mist. Return to me, for I have redeemed you. Shout for joy, O heavens, for the Lord has done it! Shout joyfully, you lower parts of the earth; Break forth into a shout of joy, you mountains, O forest, and every tree in it; for the Lord has redeemed Jacob and in Israel he shows forth his glory.
>
> Isaiah 44:22–23 (NASB)

> Break forth, shout joyfully together; for they will see with their own eyes when the Lord restores Zion. Break forth, shout joyfully together, you waste places of Jerusalem: for the Lord has comforted his people, he has redeemed Jerusalem. The Lord has bared his holy arm in the sight of all the nations, that all the ends of the earth may see the salvation of our God.
>
> Isaiah 52:9–10 (NASB)

In these passages, God speaks proudly about redeeming his people, and the ratification of the new covenant by way of the ransom is the source of his pleasure. He wants the whole earth to celebrate this redemption that he has done. This is our God visualizing the future Israel formed by those who take hold of the new covenant. There are three sources for the name "Redeemer," and they are: God redeeming Israel from Egypt for the exodus, then this ransom agreement, and the redemption of Jesus Christ who paid the price on the cross for the sin of mankind.

The use of the name "Redeemer," in Isaiah is mainly from the ransom, and is spoken of many times. Here are a few other references where the name is used: Isaiah 35:9, 41:14, 51:10, 59:20, 60:16, 62:12, 63:16, and Jeremiah 31:11. The term "redeemer" in all of these referenced passages relate to the ransom agreement by which God redeemed the new Israel. God is joyful because his plan for salvation through the new covenant had just been ratified and established throughout the heavens and the earth. It is a cause for celebration. The time of that notification made by Isaiah was about seven hundred years before the inauguration of that new covenant. Understand that the new covenant must include all of creation, both heaven and earth, which means that we must consider the spiritual realm that is not explained to us very well.

The provisions of the new covenant had a greater impact on the spiritual world than it did the physical. All of heaven, the spiritual realm, had to know all the details of the new covenant and be prepared to enforce all of the provisions demanded by it. The ransom agreement was the pivotal point around which the new covenant was ratified. In other passages of scripture that may relate to a timeframe is the period of "a time and times and half a time" used by Daniel (7:25), and in Revelation (12:14). When this ransom agreement was made, the area of the world ceded to Satan was most of the known developed world and when

PORK, BEEF, CHICKEN AND RIBS

Satan was tempting Jesus, he showed him all the kingdoms of the world. Then he said to Jesus, "I will give you all this domain and its glory; for it has been handed over to me, and I give it to whomever I wish. Therefore if you worship before me, it shall all be yours" (Luke 4:5–7 NASB).

The change in tone when God rejects the nation Israel, and when he recognizes the new Israel of God, the Christian people to come about as a result of the new covenant which had just been ratified, is very noticeable. This change takes place in the writings of Isaiah at the end of chapter 42 and the start of chapter 43. This is a pivotal point in the scriptures.

> Who gave Jacob up for spoil, and Israel to plunderers? Was it not the Lord, against whom we have sinned, and in whose ways they were not willing to walk, and whose law they did not obey? So he poured out on him the heat of his anger and the fierceness of battle; and it set him aflame all around, yet he did not recognize it; and it burned him, but he paid no attention.
>
> Isaiah 42:24–25 (NASB)

> But now, thus says the Lord, your Creator, O Jacob, and He who formed you, O Israel, do not fear, for I have redeemed you; I have called you by name; you are Mine! When you pass through the waters, I will be with you, and through the rivers, they will not overflow you. When you walk through the fire, you will not be scorched, nor will the flame burn you. For I am the Lord your God, The Holy One of Israel, your Savior; I have given Egypt as your ransom, Cush and Seba in your place. Since you are precious in my sight, since you are honored and I love you, I will give other men in your place and other peoples in exchange for your life.
>
> Isaiah 43:1–4 (NASB)

All the provisions of the new covenant have been agreed to by all of heaven and a timeline established to put it into effect. This ransom agreement ratified these provisions and is the culmination of all the planning and negotiations to bring the new covenant to fruition. The ransom is not the reason for God's joy and taken as a separate occurrence, would be distasteful. The ratification of the overall plan for salvation being offered to the entire world is the reason for God's joyful passage of Isaiah 44:23. Christians everywhere celebrate the new covenant and most without knowing its name. Even fewer would be aware that the ransom agreement was instrumental in bringing the new covenant into being.

All Christians feel the same joy for God's plan that God demonstrates in this passage, and it is cause for Christians to celebrate regardless of their knowledge of the history behind it, because they are celebrating the results of the new covenant which is their salvation gained by believing and following God's plan. There are other joyful passages throughout the remainder of Isaiah. The "Israel" God is speaking of are those who become family of God by way of the new covenant. When the new Israel is the subject, the passage is very upbeat because each person gaining their salvation through Jesus Christ is precious in God's sight.

Why has this story of the ransom agreement passed unnoticed for so many years? First the famine for the word of God was in effect until the time of the Reformation. Translation from the Hebrew language is difficult and this may have been a factor here, but a literal translation telling of God ceding a part of the world, along with the people within that area to Satan is unthinkable in the minds of almost everyone. I believe that anything written in the Bible is there by God's wishes, for a purpose, and we should attempt to understand it without formula or special abilities. God has promised us that before he does anything, he lets it be known to his prophets, who are then required to tell his plans to the people. God has also told us that he does nothing in secret and that reinforces the idea that all scriptures must be understandable by any person willing to study; and studying the scriptures is required because God has also said that his people are destroyed for lack of knowledge.

Apostle Paul, in his letter to Timothy (2 Tim. 3:16), says that all scriptures are inspired by God. The only other power to which a ransom could be paid is Satan. This fact alone prohibits most theologians from accepting the literal translation, even though there are several passages supporting it. A possible reason that this passage has not been publicized is that the ransom looks to be the primary subject when the redemption is the true cause for celebration. This redemption when spoken of in Jeremiah 31:11 states that God redeemed his people from the hand of him who was stronger than them. A literal interpretation of this passage is substantiated by what Satan said to Jesus during the temptation. Read that passage again for it is important.

> And he led Him up and showed Him all the kingdoms of the world in a moment of time. And the devil said to Him, "I will give you all this domain and its glory; for it as been handed over to me, and I give it to whomever I wish. Therefore, if You worship before me, it shall all be Yours.
>
> Luke 4: 5–7 (NASB)

In an attempt to validate my interpretation of the book of Isaiah, I studied three different commentaries on Isaiah 43:1—7. None of the three give the ransom passage the importance it deserves. One commentary writes off a literal interpretation of the ransom agreement by saying: "an excessively literal reading raises some theological questions about God's indiscriminate condemning of surrounding nations merely to get Israel off the hook."

One commentary continues with the statement: "Many commentators maintain that Cyrus is being promised the prize—rule of the lush Nile valley in return for allowing the Jews to return home." None of the commentaries mention the other party to the ransom agreement, which to my belief must be Satan. I believe that God is relinquishing his activity within those countries named in the passage, and in return he gets some agreement that is very pleasing to him.

None of the commentaries address the concept that this passage is initiating a new and different relationship between God and mankind, which is the most important aspect of Isaiah 1–7. These commentaries are compiled from the efforts of many Christian theologians, and guidelines were necessary to establish how the interpretations would be accomplished. I am thankful that these guidelines are set forth in the General Editor's preface of the book because the guidelines require the interpretation of scripture set forth in the book to be irenic in tone (non-controversial).

For the resulting interpretations to be non-controversial, it is necessary that the outcome of the combined effort be commonly acceptable interpretation, which can be used by many denominations. I am interested in reformed Christian interpretation, and the controversy is a nonissue. The scripture, telling about the ransom paid to Satan, is probably the most controversial, which eliminates or at least limits discussion of it from the commentaries. I believe that this story of the ransom agreement is the most significant passage in Isaiah because it marks the turning point in God's plan of salvation, which makes his salvation available to the entire world. This magnificent story is not new but has been obscured throughout most of the last two thousand years, because the famine for the Word of God was in effect for most of this time, and some confusion is brought about by the new covenant family of God being called by the same name as the ancestral nation Israel.

> But now, thus says the Lord, your Creator, O Jacob, and he who formed you, O Israel, "Do not fear, for I have redeemed you; I have called you by name; you are mine!
>
> Isaiah 43:1 (NASB)

The words "formed you, O Israel," is indicative of those people of the new covenant, are tested, and refined, or formed, as described in Zechariah 13:9 (the refining process). Isaiah uses the same words to describe the new Israel in 43:7. To redeem implies a payment has been made to retrieve something; and here it is, the new Israel that has been redeemed. It is this act that has caused God to refer to himself as the Redeemer. "I have called you by name; you are mine," denotes ownership and a family relationship through the name. The prophesy about the new covenant at Jer. 33:16 gives the name, "The Lord is our righteousness," to the new Israel. Isaiah 43:7 reads, "Everyone who is called by my name."

> When you pass through the waters, I will be with you; And through the rivers, they will not overflow you. When you walk through the fire, you will not be scorched, nor will the flame burn you.
>
> Isaiah 43:2 (NASB)

This passage relate to the known power of God to hold back the water for Moses, Elijah, Elisha, and Joshua. It also relates directly to God's refining process from Zechariah.

> It will come about in all the land," declares the Lord, "that two parts in it will be cut off and perish; but the third will be left in it. And I will bring the third part through the fire, refine them as silver is refined, and test them as gold is tested. They will call on my name, and I will answer them; I will say, 'they are my people,' and they will say, 'The Lord is my God.'
>
> Zechariah 13:9 (NASB)

God is using a metaphor to describe the testing that you or I might be subjected to in our everyday lives. Assume that you are faced with the possibility of receiving a large sum of money, but you must tell a lie to receive it. You may be in God's refining process, and if you refuse to lie, you gain value in God's eyes. If you lie to receive the wealth, then you have been burned; you have been set aflame without recognizing the damage which it will cause you. The metaphor of refining and testing gold and silver is used when the testing of God's people is the subject. Gold was tested by submerging it in water to determine its volume by measuring the amount of water displaced, and then floating it in a vessel to determine its weight by the amount of water displaced by the vessel, and then the specific gravity of the gold could be computed. The process of refining gold and silver involved heating the ore by fire until the metal liquifies and will pour away from the dross. This testing us like gold is tested, and refining us as silver is refined, is promised by God, and is the source for the wording in Isaiah 43:2. Note also that this statement that the flame will not burn you is different from that similar statement speaking of the nation Israel, where they were burned by the flame, but paid it no attention.

> Who gave Jacob up for spoil, and Israel to plunderers? Was it not the Lord, against whom we have sinned, and in whose ways they were not willing to walk, And whose law they did not obey? So He poured out on him the heat of his anger and the fierceness of battle; and it set him aflame all around, yet he did not recognize it; and it burned him, but he paid no attention.
>
> Isaiah 42:24–25 (NASB)

Here we see that the nation Israel was unaware of the heat from God's refining process. God does not say anything about a flame in the burning because Jacob would not walk in his ways.

> For I am the Lord your God, The Holy One of Israel, your Savior; I have given Egypt as your ransom, Cush and Seba in your place. Since you are precious in my sight, Since you are honored and I love you, I will give other men in your place and other peoples in exchange for your life.
>
> Isaiah 43:3–4 (NASB)

Here, God explains what the ransom payment included, and calls the names of three nations which were given over to another in the ransom agreement. Then God tells his reason for taking this action: "Since you are precious in my sight, since you are honored and I love you." This statement places the redeemed within the bonds of the new covenant, and does so unequivocally. The redeemed are those who are his possession and all of creation knows this because of their name. Then a shift to future tense; "I will give," denotes a future action and a description of what was paid as ransom is clearly stated as men exchanged for the men being redeemed. The new covenant with the universe has been ratified, but the activity to give others in exchange for the redeemed, is to take place in the future. This future tense is common for the provisions or changes prophesied to occur in conjunction with the new covenant.

The three nations given as ransom covered the Middle East at the time of the Jewish captivity in Babylon. Seba or Sheba was located where Yemen is today and its capital was Marib. The trade in frankincense and myrrh made the country very rich, and their trade routes extended from the Indian Ocean to the Mediterranean Sea. No other government entity, other than Sheba, existed in the Arabian Peninsula during the reign of King Nebuchadnezzar, of the Chaldeans, when Israel was conquered and carried into captivity to Babylon. The Chaldeans continued their conquest to include much of Egypt. After the death of Nebuchadnezzar in 562 BC, the influence of the Chaldean

Empire decreased under the reign of his son Belshazzar, and in 539 BC, the Persian Empire under Cyrus, conquered the entire Chaldean Empire. Egypt became a part of the Persian Empire, and Darius (Dan. 9:1), the successor to Cyrus, was called Pharaoh. The Egypt named in Isa. 43:2 was apparently constituted by this larger Persian Empire ruled by Darius I, who was King of Persia and also the Pharaoh of Egypt.

At the time of the ransom agreement, the countries given in payment constituted most all the world as it was known at that time. The Isaiah commentaries that I have read give Cyrus as recipient of the ransom. This concept would have elevated Cyrus to a very imposing position with God, but this concept appears to be eliminated by Isa. 45:13 which reads: "I have aroused him in righteousness and I will make all his ways smooth; he will build my city and will let my exiles go free, without any payment or reward, says the Lord of host." Here the person being discussed is Cyrus, and he received no payment or reward for releasing Israel from captivity in Egypt. Since the ransom was a payment or reward, the Isaiah commentary is proven inaccurate by this passage.

The ransom appears to be for a period of time corresponding with the famine for the Word of God. Both of these prophesies were fulfilled over the same period and appear to have begun in the first or second century and lasted until the Reformation. There had to be a timeline established for the changes to occur and all the heavenly beings had to be committed to that timetable. Jesus was aware of the timeline when he told his mother at the wedding in Cana that his hour had not yet come. God is elated following the culmination of planning to bring about his new covenant, and there are other passages that confirm his pleasure:

> For the Lord has ransomed Jacob and redeemed him from the hand of him who was stronger than he.
>
> Jeremiah 31:11 (NASB)

PORK, BEEF, CHICKEN AND RIBS

> Remember these things O Jacob, and Israel, for you are my servant; I have formed you, you are my servant, O Israel, you will not be forgotten by me. I have wiped out your transgressions like a thick cloud and your sins like a heavy mist. Return to me for I have redeemed you." Shout for joy, O heavens, for the Lord has done it! Shout joyfully, you lower parts of the earth; break forth into a shout of joy, you mountains, O forest, and every tree in it; for the Lord has redeemed Jacob and in Israel he shows forth his glory.
>
> Isaiah 44: 21–24 (NASB)

> For a brief moment I forsook you, but with great compassion I will gather you. In an outburst of anger I hid my face from you for a moment, but with everlasting loving-kindness I will have compassion on you, says the Lord your Redeemer." "For this is like the days of Noah to me, when I swore that the waters of Noah would not flood the earth again; so I have sworn that I will not be angry with you nor will I rebuke you.
>
> Isaiah 54:7–9 (NASB)

Following the ratification of the new covenant and the joyful passages following it, God speaks through Isaiah the strongest warning to us that he does not change. These warnings are designed to deter people from worshipping a deity demonstrating different qualities than those demonstrated by him. He may change his mind as a result of our fervent prayers, such as giving Hezekiah fifteen more years to live (2 Kings 20:6), but his character is steadfast. To many it will be inconceivable that God would give lives of other people for the purpose of ratifying the new covenant; but remember, God values our spiritual lives and knows that this life is not to be desired when compared to our heavenly existence.

The ransom that God paid for the new Israel established an area of the world to be controlled by Satan, and facilitated a distinct geographical separation between the People of God, and the people of Satan. Satan established a religion where he would be worshipped and his ways considered right, and it renounces Christianity, or God's plan. The apostle Paul told us that a renunciation of our religion must precede the return of Jesus Christ. He referred to this renunciation as an apostasy. There is no other apostasy mentioned in the writings incorporated into the New Testament, nor is there any force other than the Islamic religion that renounces Christianity. Paul is authoritative because he is an apostle selected by the risen Christ and also taught by him. Now read that prophetic writing from Paul which tells about the evil force to come which will renounce the Christian religion. Paul was writing in the first century and the apostasy occurred post seventh century.

> Now we request you, brethren, with regard to the coming of our Lord Jesus Christ and our gathering together to Him, that you not be quickly shaken from your composure or be disturbed either by a spirit or a message or a letter as if from us, to the effect that the day of the Lord has come.
>
> Let no one in any way deceive you, for it will not come unless the apostasy comes first, and the man of lawlessness is revealed, the son of destruction, who opposes and exalts himself above every so-called god or object of worship, so that he takes his seat in the temple of God, displaying himself as being God.
>
> Do you not remember that while I was still with you, I was telling you these things? And you know what restrains him now, so that in his time he will be revealed. For the mystery of lawlessness is already at work; only he who now restrains will do so until he is taken out of the way.
>
> Then that lawless one will be revealed whom the Lord will slay with the breath of His mouth and bring to an end by the appearance of His coming; that is the one whose coming is in accord with the activity of Satan,

with all power and signs and false wonders, and with all the deception of wickedness for those who perish, because they did not receive the love of the truth so as to be saved. For this reason God will send upon them a deluding influence so that they will believe what is false, in order that they all may be judged who did not believe the truth, but took pleasure in wickedness.

2 Thessalonians 2:1–12 (NASB)

The word "apostasy" used in the NASB, was interpreted as "a falling away," in the KJV and probably other versions of the Bible as well. This new rendering is more exact. The "Apostasy," told about by Paul requires a renunciation of Christianity by a major force, and must also involve theology. Since this apostasy will be observable by all Christians, it must be widespread and recognizable.

The Jews denied the divinity of Christ because he came without being like they expected, and this difference of opinion existed as Paul was writing, so they cannot be considered the apostasy. The only situation that fulfills Paul's apostasy is the rise of Islam and the Muslim religion. The opposing theology is involved and the whole of Christianity was aware of the competing force; and they reacted by military action, the crusades, against the intruding power. The crusades were unsuccessful because of logistics, but the advance of Islam was slowed.

Islam is the only world power that promotes a theology that is diametrically opposed to Christianity, and Paul refers to this theology as lawlessness, because it professes rules to live by that are opposite what Jesus taught and what God has published in the Bible. The Muslims are taught that they worship the same god that Jews and Christians worship. In the Koran, at Sura (chapter) 3, verses 1 and 2, the God of the Koran claims to be the only god and claims to have "sent down the Law and the

Evangel (previous scripture) aforetime, as man's guidance." Thus the Muslims are taught that their god is the same deity that was worshipped by Abraham, Moses, the Jews, and the Christians. Nothing could be farther from the truth.

When I look at the obvious anti-Christian teachings in the Koran, I am surprised that the Christian community has not spoken out loudly that the god of the Koran is not the same god as our God. There has been a lack of study within the Christian community on the teachings of Islam. Regardless of what the world calls Islam or what it names itself—it is a cult, the world's largest cult.

Look at the design of it, and see that it meets every requirement in mind control of its followers, and in the social mores necessary for membership. Membership is not optional and a member cannot leave the foal and live. Paul's description of the force that will renounce Christianity, says that "God will send a deluding influence so that they will believe what is false," adequately explains the mind control or "brainwashing" accomplished by the application of teachings from the Koran.

The Koran describes a Christian as "one who joins other gods with God." Mohammad coined this descriptive phrase because of the Christian belief in the deity of Christ and the Holy Spirit. The God to whom we join Christ and the Holy Spirit is the God of the Bible. The teachings of the Koran prove that the God of the Bible is not the God of the Koran, because the teachings are very different.

THE APOSTLE PAUL

Because prophesy made by Apostle Paul is of major importance to the Christian belief, one must be aware of the divine authority placed on this man. Paul was first known as Saul of Tarsus. Tarsus was an important Roman city in the province of Cilicia, in Asia Minor. His birth there made him a Roman citizen, and the affluent area provided good educational opportunities. Saul was apparently sent to Jerusalem as a teenager to study under Gamaliel, which indicates that he came from a prominent Jewish family background. I want to emphasize the divine authority bestowed on Apostle Paul, so it is necessary that you know the call that the Lord placed on Saul of Tarsus who became Apostle Paul. Apostle Paul was taught by Jesus and was shown visions of what was to happen in future times. We should accept that what Paul wrote for us as truth. Apostle Paul also said that all scriptures are inspired by God (2 Tim. 3:16). Apostle Paul was taught by Jesus Christ directly, according to his report made in Galatians.

> For I would have you know, brethren, that the gospel which was preached by me is not according to man. For I neither received it from man, nor was I taught it, but I received it through a revelation of Jesus Christ.
>
> Galatians 1:11–12 (NASB)

He was also shown visions which caused him to describe them at 2 Cor. 12:7 with the passage "Because of the surpassing greatness of the revelations." Apostle Paul also explained the influence of the devil on those who did not understand the Gospel of Jesus Christ, and said that he had blinded their minds. In this passage, the unbelieving are the non-Christians.

> And even if our gospel is veiled, it is veiled to those who are perishing, in whose case the god of this world has blinded the minds of the unbelieving so that they might not see the light of the gospel of the glory of Christ, who is the image of God. For we do not preach ourselves but Christ Jesus as Lord, and ourselves as your bond-servants for Jesus's sake. For God, who said, "Light shall shine out of darkness," is the one who has shone in our hearts to give the light of the knowledge of the glory of God in the face of Christ.
>
> 2 Corinthians 4:3–8 (NASB)

Saul is first mentioned in Acts 7:58, when he looked after the coats of those stoning Stephen to death for professing Jesus as the Christ and as divine. Following the death of Stephen, Saul would become the most rabid prosecutor of the new Christian church, and was in the process of seeking out the followers of Christ, when Jesus called upon him to be his disciple. Paul's own words tell the story:

> I am a Jew, born in Tarsus of Cilicia, but brought up in this city, educated under Gamaliel, strictly according to the law of our fathers, being zealous for God just as you all are today. I persecuted this Way to the death, binding and putting both men and women into prisons, as also the high priest and all the Council of the Elders can testify. From them I also received letters to the brethren and started off for Damascus in order to bring even those who were there to Jerusalem as prisoners to be punished.

PORK, BEEF, CHICKEN AND RIBS

But it happened that as I was on my way, approaching Damascus about noontime, a very bright light suddenly flashed from heaven all around me, and I fell to the ground and heard a voice saying to me, 'Saul, Saul, why are you persecuting me?' And I answered, 'Who are you, Lord?'

And he said to me, 'I am Jesus the Nazarene, whom you are persecuting.' And those who were with me saw the light, to be sure, but did not understand the voice of the one who was speaking to me.

And I said, 'What shall I do, Lord?' And the Lord said to me, 'Get up and go on into Damascus, and there you will be told of all that has been appointed for you to do.'

But since I could not see because of the brightness of that light, I was led by the hand by those who were with me and came into Damascus. A certain Ananias, a man who was devout by standard of the Law, and well spoken of by all the Jews who lived there, came to me, and standing near said to me, 'Brother Saul, receive your sight!'

And at that very time I looked up at him. And he said, 'The God of our fathers has appointed you to know his will and to see the Righteous One and to hear an utterance from his mouth. For you will be a witness for him to all men of what you have seen and heard. Now why do you delay? Get up and be baptized, and wash away your sins, calling on his name.'

It happened when I returned to Jerusalem and was praying in the temple, that I fell into a trance, and I saw him saying to me, 'Make haste, and get out of Jerusalem quickly, because they will not accept your testimony about me.' And I said, "Lord, they themselves understand that in one synagogue after another I used to imprison and beat those who believed in you. And when the blood of your witness Stephen was being shed, I also was standing by approving, and watching out for the coats of those who were slaying him." And he said to me, Go! for I will send you far away to the Gentiles.'

Acts 22:3–21 (NASB)

Paul became the disciple to the Gentiles and the most dedicated worker in the early Christian church. The time span from the time Saul, as a youth, was holding the coats of the devout Jews stoning Stephen to death, and the time Jesus called him to be a disciple on the road to Damascus, was probably about twelve years. Luke describes the Lord's call made to Paul:

> Now Saul, still breathing threats and murder against the disciples of the Lord, went to the high priest and asked for letters from him to the synagogues at Damascus, so that if he found any belonging to the Way, both men and women, he might bring them bound to Jerusalem. As he was traveling, it happened that he was approaching Damascus, and suddenly a light from heaven flashed around him, and he fell to the ground and heard a voice saying to him, "Saul, Saul, why are you persecuting me?" And he said, "Who are you Lord?" and He said;, "I am Jesus whom you are persecuting, but get up and enter the city and it will be told you what you must do."
>
> The men who traveled with him stood speechless, hearing the voice but seeing no one. Saul got up from the ground, and though his eyes were open, he could see nothing; and leading him by the hand, they brought him into Damascus. And he was three days without sight, and neither ate nor drank.
>
> Now there was a disciple at Damascus named Ananias; and the Lord said to him in a vision, "Ananias." And he said, "Here I am Lord." And the Lord said to him, "Get up and go to the street called Straight, and inquire at the house of Judas for a man from Tarsus named Saul, for he is praying, and he has seen in a vision a man named Ananias come in and lay his hands on him, so that he might regain his sight." But Ananias answered, "Lord I have heard from many about this man, how much harm he did to your saints at Jerusalem; and here he has authority from the chief priests to bind all who call on your name."

> But the Lord said to him, "Go, for he is a chosen instrument of mine, to bear my name before the Gentiles and kings and the sons of Israel, for I will show him how much he must suffer for my name's sake."
> So Ananias departed and entered the house, and after laying his hands on him said, "Brother Saul, The Lord Jesus, who appeared to you on the road by which you were coming, has sent me so that you may regain your sight and be filled with the Holy Spirit." And immediately there fell from his eyes something like scales, and he regained his sight, and he got up and was baptized, and he took food and was strengthened.
> Now for several days he was with the disciples who were at Damascus, and Immediately, he began to proclaim Jesus in the synagogues, saying, "He is the Son of God." All those hearing him continued to be amazed, and were saying, Is this not he who in Jerusalem destroyed those who called on this name, and who had come here for the purpose of bringing them bound before the chief priest?" But Saul kept increasing in strength and confounding the Jews who lived at Damascus by proving that this Jesus is the Christ. When many days had elapsed, the Jews plotted together to do away with him, but their plot became known to Saul. They were also watching the gates day and night so that they might put him to death, but his disciples took him by night and let him down through an opening in the wall, lowering him in a large basket.
>
> Acts 9: 1–25 (NASB)

After his escape from Damascus, Paul returned to Arabia, likely to his hometown of Tarsus. Paul does not tell the length of time he remained in Tarsus, but three years is the suspected interval of time. During this stay in Tarsus, Paul received revelations from the Lord and was given knowledge which he describes as inexpressible. He was apparently taken up into heaven, probably in spirit, and heard inexpressible words that he is not allowed to speak, and shown things that must occur, and shown how the return of Jesus Christ will progress. Paul tells of this experience.

> In Damascus, the ethnarch, under Aretas the king was guarding the city of the Damascenes in order to seize me, and I was let down in a basket through a window in the wall, and so escaped his hands. Boasting is necessary, though it is not profitable; but I will go on to visions and revelations of the Lord. I know a man in Christ who fourteen years ago—whether in body I do not know, or out of the body I do not know, God knows —such a man was caught up to the third heaven. And I know how such a man—whether in the body apart from the body I do not know, God knows—was caught up into Paradise and heard inexpressible words, which a man is not permitted to speak. On behalf of such a man I will boast; but on my own behalf I will not boast, except in regard to my weakness. For if I do wish to boast I will not be foolish, for I will be speaking the truth; but I refrain from this, so that no one will credit me with more than he sees in me or hears from me. Because of the surpassing greatness of the revelations, for this reason, to keep me from exalting myself, there was given me a thorn in the flesh, a messenger of Satan to torment me—to keep me from exalting myself!
>
> 2 Corinthians 11:32 to 12:7 (NASB)

We learn more about Paul's visions in his letter to the Galatians. The gospel that he was to preach was shown him through revelations of Jesus Christ. Paul tells about these revelations.

> For I would have you know, brethren, that the gospel which was preached by me is not according to man. For I neither received it from man, nor was I taught it, but I received it through a revelation of Jesus Christ. For you have heard

of my former manner of life in Judaism, how I used to persecute the church of God beyond measure and tried to destroy it; and I was advancing in Judaism beyond many of my contemporaries among my countrymen, being more extremely zealous for my ancestral traditions. But when God, who had set me apart even from my mother's womb and called me through his grace, was pleased to reveal his Son in me so that I might preach him among the Gentiles, I did not immediately consult with flesh and blood, nor did I go up to Jerusalem to those who were apostles before me; but I went away to Arabia, and returned once more to Damascus. Then three years later I went up to Jerusalem, to become acquainted with Cephas, and stayed with him fifteen days.

Galatians 1:11–18 (NASB)

Not since Moses had there been so much communication from heaven directed to an individual. Apostle Paul rightly holds great respect within Christianity, and his prophesy regarding the end-times should not be questioned. Notice here that Paul informs us that this teaching is "by the word of the Lord." Here are other scriptures where Paul was in communication with the Lord (Acts 16:9, 18:9, 19:6, 23:11, 27:9, 24).

But we do not want you to be uninformed, brethren, about those who are asleep, so that you will not grieve as do the rest who have no hope. For if we believe that Jesus died and rose again, even so God will bring with Him those who have fallen asleep in Jesus. For this we say to you by the word of the Lord, that we who are alive and remain until the coming of the Lord, will not precede those who have fallen asleep. For the Lord Himself will descend from heaven with a shout, with the voice of the archangel and with the trumpet of God, and the dead in Christ will rise first. Then we who are alive and remain will be caught up together with them in the clouds to meet the Lord in the air, and so we shall always be with the Lord. Therefore comfort one another with these words.

1 Thessalonians 4:13–17 (NASB)

Christians periodically profess their faith in Jesus by re-enacting the Lord's Supper by the act called "communion." Apostle Paul tells of the Lord's request that we do this. Notice here that Paul states that he received this instruction from the Lord. Paul was not with Jesus while he was alive on the earth; therefore, this teaching had to come from the visions or teachings from the risen Lord while Paul was sequestered in Arabia (Likely in his hometown in Tarsus) following his escape from Damascus.

> For I received from the Lord that which I also delivered to you, that the Lord Jesus in the night in which he was betrayed took bread; and when he had given thanks, he broke it and said, "This is my body, which is for you; do this in remembrance of me." In the same way he took the cup also after supper, saying, "This cup is the new covenant in my blood; do this, as often as you drink it, in remembrance of me." For as often as you eat this bread and drink the cup, you proclaim the Lord's death until he comes. Therefore whoever eats the bread and drinks the cup of the Lord in an unworthy manner, shall be guilty of the body and the blood of the Lord. But a man must examine himself, and in so doing he is to eat of the bread and drink of the cup. For he who eats and drinks, eats and drinks judgement to himself if he does not judge the body rightly.
>
> 1 Corinthians 11: 23–29 (NASB)

The warning given by Paul is for those people who have joined in the meal for the nourishment and do not believe in the Lord Jesus. During Paul's time the communion meal must have consisted of much more bread and wine than what we use today as a symbol of the original meal. Paul's warning is for us to do a self check on our faith. If we believe in the Lord and wish to please him; recognizing that the bread and wine symbolizes his body broken for us, and his blood poured out on the cross, then we participate in the communion meal. It is important that all realize that the communion meal was requested by the Lord when he said, "do this in remembrance of me." Some people will refrain from partaking of the communion meal because they feel guilty for some sin they have committed. God has promised to forget our sins; therefore, all that is necessary to remove the guilt is to ask for God's forgiveness, and then participate in the meal to affirm your faith.

The most important revelation that Apostle Paul made was about the apostasy that must occur before the Lord returns. This passage was written earlier but the importance of it requires added attention.

> Now, we request you, brethren, with regard to the coming of our Lord Jesus Christ and our gathering together to him, that you not be quickly shaken from your composure or be disturbed either by a spirit or a message or a letter as if from us, to the effect that the day of the Lord has come. Let no one in any way deceive you, for it will not come unless the apostasy comes first, and the man of lawlessness is revealed, the son of destruction, who opposes and exalts himself above every so-called god or object of worship, so that he takes his seat in the temple of God, displaying himself as being God. Do you not remember that while I was still with you, I was telling you these things? And you know what restrains him now, so that in his time he will be revealed. For the mystery of lawlessness is already at work; only he who now restrains will do so until he is taken out of the way. Then that lawless one will be revealed whom the Lord will slay with the breath of his mouth and bring to an end by the appearance of his coming; that is the

one whose coming is in accord with the activity of Satan, with all power and signs and false wonders, and with all the deception of wickedness for those who perish, because they did not receive the love of the truth so as to be saved. For this reason God will send upon them a deluding influence so that they will believe what is false, in order that they all may be judged who did not believe the truth, but took pleasure in wickedness.

2 Thessalonians 2:1–12 (NASB)

This passage has not received the attention that it deserves because the Greek word "Apostica" was translated incorrectly in the King James Version of the Bible. The English word is "apostasy" and the primary meaning is renunciation of a religious faith. The secondary meaning is abandonment of a previous loyalty. The King James Version used the secondary meaning by saying "a falling away" as if Christians themselves would abandon the religion. It becomes obvious that the "Apostasy" spoken of by Paul is the book of Islam, the Koran. The description of the one who opposes is proof enough that this conclusion is correct. Every attribute espoused in the Bible to be worthy of attainment is redirected to an opposite view or distorted in the Koran, and it establishes a cult-like religious order designed for the sole purpose of opposing Christianity.

THE SPIRITUAL REALM

There comes a time in everyone's life when they must reflect on their past and determine whether they have had a good impact on this world—whether they have accomplished any good thing or not. With old age comes the idea that they have gained some wisdom and then comes the desire to pass along the knowledge they have gained for the benefit of their offsprings or anyone else that they might reach. That is where I find myself as I approach the time when I must enter into my rest. I was brought up going to church and became a Christian at an early age; however, I did not join the church until I was older and after an exciting career as an Air Force fighter pilot and Flying Safety Officer. At the time I became a follower of Christ, I was thirty-six years of age and was inspired by God in a dream, to change my sinful life and to follow ways pleasing to him.

I write this treatise with the express knowledge that it is what God desires me to do. While I came to know God at an early age, I did not join with the church because of bad theology that had been preached from the same pulpit to which I answered his call. While my desired audience to read this treatise is my family and my fellow Christians, I sincerely hope that all people seeking to know God will benefit from it. When my desire to write this book reached its climax, I was convinced that many so called religions, failed to provide the salvation promised by its teachings and I wanted to warn everyone that I could reach with the religious knowledge that I have gained after forty-five years of study.

My decision was finalized while driving through rural Alabama, when I saw an abandoned barbecue pit advertising the four types of fare that had once been provided there. The sign was painted on the large chimney rising over the pit where the meats were cooked. The sign was in very good condition, so I was surprised to learn that the building which had housed the restaurant had burned five years earlier. This advertisement caught my eye because it was so obviously misleading; the business establishment necessary to provide the food advertised was missing. My thought at the time was that this barbecue pit is proclaiming a cuisine that is just not there; and in a similar manner, there are many religions that promise a way to God that are empty of any such benefit. I did not think that many people would be attracted to a book titled "Comparative Religions," but I thought that a title of "Pork, Beef, Chicken, and Ribs," would attract attention and a picture of this abandoned barbecue pit could provide the cover.

I have studied different religions for the last forty-five years in order to distinguish which is good and which is not. I have studied the history of religions along with study of the Bible which is the basis for most all religious beliefs. I have studied secular history and find that those prophesies made in the Bible have been fulfilled in the world. Since 2000 I have read the Koran more than ten times and scrutinized many parts of it, and noted news articles relating to Islam for the past fifteen years. What I have learned has astounded me. Islam was devised to oppose Christianity. I will show the opposing views by using the words from the Koran and from the Bible, and give you some surprising insight resulting from forty-five years of study, regarding religion.

I truly feel that I have learned the correct image of God, the God of the Bible, for he has given me many blessings from our relationship. God is not overbearing, or even obvious to most people, and that makes it easy to overlook his presence in today's busy world with confusing theological competition. God's power is unfathomable and he is working his plan in our world today in powerful ways. This abandoned barbecue pit advertising a non-existent menu has goaded me to write my personal message while there is still time. I hope that this effort will cause others to find a good relationship with God. I speak about the Almighty God; the God of Abraham, and Isaac, and Jacob; who spoke with Moses from a burning bush some three thousand five hundred years ago, and inspired him to record the history of his people in the Pentateuch, that scripture of old, that is sometimes referred to as the, "Book of Moses."

The most common method of seeking God is meditation, so find a place where you are comfortable; a place where you can reflect upon your life and the meaning of life. Dedicate the place selected as your holy ground for your time of meditation. When God attracted Moses to a burning bush that was not being consumed, he told Moses to remove his sandals because he was standing on holy ground. (Ex. 3:5) That is an indication to me that any place where you meet God is holy ground. Concentrate on whatever troubles you most, and ask God to provide you with some relief from that problem. The most common proof of the spiritual realm is answered prayer. Continue to seek his help and watch for your relief to come. Miracles do happen, but do not expect one to happen because often a person does not recognize that one has occurred until long afterwards. If relief does not come for you, try again and again.

Jesus told Nicodemus that a person must be born of the spirit in order to see the kingdom of God. (John 3:3 NASB). This discussion with Nicodemus results in Jesus saying the most popular passage in the New Testament: "For God so loved the world that he gave his only begotten Son, that whoever believes in him shall not perish, but have eternal life" (John 3:16 NASB) This then is what is meant by being "born again" whoever believes in "him" the only begotten Son, Jesus. Similar words with the same description of "born again", comes at John 6:40 when Jesus says; "for this is the will of my Father, that everyone who beholds the Son and believes in him will have eternal life." After the spiritual rebirth or spiritual awakening, a believer may be baptized in order to be symbolically cleansed from sin. Following Paul's conversion on the road to Damascus, Ananias revealed to him what God had instructed and then added; "Now, why do you delay? Get up and be baptized, and wash away your sins, calling on his name."

Jesus told the woman of Samaria at the well (John 4:24 NASB): "God is spirit, and those who worship him must worship in spirit and truth." God is a spirit, and a part of you will become spirit when your physical life on this earth is over, and that part is called the soul.

This is not my intuition but the teachings from God that I have learned from study of his Word. The writings in the Bible profess to be teachings from God and necessarily originate within the spiritual realm. In the New American Standard Bible, the version from which I quote in this writing, the word "heaven" which refers to our place of residence after we leave this physical life, is used 640 times. Other words which usually refer to the spiritual realm are used numerous times. "Spirit" is used 591 times; "righteousness" is used 595 times; "faith" 493; and "believe" 284. The Apostle Paul describing our spiritual life wrote: "While we look not at the things which are seen, but at the things which are not seen; for the things which are seen are temporal, but the things which are not seen are eternal" (2 Cor. 4:18 NASB). The eleventh chapter of Hebrews begins by: "Now faith is the assurance of things hoped for, the conviction of things not seen.

For by it the men of old gained approval. By faith we understand that the worlds were prepared by the word of God, so that what is seen was not made out of things which are visible" (Hebrews 11:1–2 NASB). The worlds are heaven, the spiritual realm; and earth, the physical realm. If we believe the Bible, then it naturally follows that we also believe in the spiritual realm.

Jesus told that, "as Moses lifted up the serpent in the wilderness, even so must The Son of Man be lifted up, so that whoever believes will in him have eternal life" (John 3:14–15, NASB). This lifting up was accomplished by the Romans when they lifted him up on the cross to crucify him. The historical occurrence that Jesus was referring to was the cure which God provided the Hebrew people who were bitten during the plague of poisonous serpents during their exodus from Egypt. In the wilderness God brought a plague of poisonous snakes upon the rebellious Hebrew people, and he then told Moses to make a likeness of the serpent and place it on a pole, and those who were bitten could look upon the likeness of the serpent and live (Num. 21:6–9 NASB). The act of looking upon the bronze serpent in order to be saved was an act of faith by those bitten; therefore, they were saved from death by their faith in God to save them. In a similar manner a Christian is eternally saved by faith in Jesus to accomplish their salvation.

God wants all humankind to live in peace, and be free to choose their own destiny, and wants us to love justice. This is God's teaching that all humankind are born with certain inalienable rights, which are the right to live and not be killed in infancy by any religion, disease, strife or starvation; and the right to be free from fear of anyone, or any government, or any organization; and the right to seek a life of happiness on this earth regardless of the color of our skin, or the wealth of our family, or our sexual identity; and regardless of whether we are born American, Hebrew, Hindu, or Hutu. If you truly want to live a life acceptable to God, you must only want to do what is right and desire justice for everyone. These two requirements are what God has said, you must love justice and righteousness; and righteousness is simply doing what is right. Do you want to take advantage of someone? If so, then you do not love justice. Will you lie in order to impress someone or to make a profit? If so, you do not want what is right. Do you want to impose your will on anyone by force? If so, then you seek what is evil. In order to please God your scales must be accurate, and your thoughts without bias.

The spiritual realm is populated by both good and evil spirits and prior to the coming of Jesus the separation between the physical and the spiritual worlds were not as great as after his coming. The new covenant, which was for the salvation of anyone, anywhere in the world, required that the power exercised by the spiritual beings be curtailed. Read now of the changes that were to come that were written about five hundred years before Jesus was born.

> It will come about in that day" declares the Lord of hosts, "That I will cut off the names of the idols from the land, and they will no longer be remembered: and I will also remove the prophets and the unclean spirit from the land.
>
> Zechariah 13:2 (NASB)

The term "in that day", denotes the time when the new covenant God made with the worlds would come about, and Jesus was the person who ushered in that new covenant. The change in the relationship between the spiritual realm and the physical world or the interaction between the two is very important to understanding the provisions that God has included in his new covenant. It is my opinion that the forces of evil hold a greater advantage under the old system and would have resisted the implementation of the new covenant. Evidence of the Spiritual realm is plentiful throughout the Bible so please be cognizant of that as you study. The Koran originated from the spiritual realm according to what was told by Muhammad, and I see evidence to support that belief. I will report my findings from study of the Koran next, because most people reading this epistle will be Christian and more interested to learn why I say that Islam was devised to oppose Christianity. I also want the Muslim reader to recognize that I have expended much effort studying the Koran and do not want to offend the Muslim readers who will benefit from this book.

THE KORAN

INTRODUCTION

During the formative years for the church, the eastern branch from Constantinople (Now Istanbul, Turkey) became increasingly different from Rome, and succumbed to heresies that weakened the faith through disputes about the nature of Christ. Constantinople and the Eastern division of Christianity including Asia Minor, and the Middle East, became embroiled in conflicting ideas of the nature of Jesus. The Christians thought him to be *divine*, but the Jews and Gnostic religions denied his divinity and some strange heresies resulted from these theological differences. The Gnostic Valentinus, who claimed to have been instructed by Theodas, a disciple of Paul, wrote: "Jesus ate and drank in a peculiar manner, not evacuating his food. So much power of continence was in him that in him his food was not corrupted, since he himself had no corruptibility." (Paul Johnson, "A History of Christianity," Atheneum, New York 1980, p. 89) After the church at Rome banished Nestorius to Syria in 433, the Nestorian sect worked diligently to build their own churches, schools, and seminaries. The Nestorians adamantly professed that Jesus was only human. There are several ancient writings said to be associated with the early Christian church that are likely products of the Nestorians. These writings originated in Coptic, the language of Egypt and likely Syria of that day, which makes them suspect of being heresy. It was this weakness in the eastern church of this time, that facilitated the acceptance of the Muslim model throughout the Middle East. Remember also that the scriptures were available to the priest only, and were only supposed to be read in Latin.

The teachings of the Koran denies the basic tenants of Christianity, which are that Jesus Christ, who was God in the flesh, was made a sacrifice for the sins of the world and that he was crucified on the cross, was dead, and buried; and the third day he rose from the dead; and now is alive and sits by the Father in heaven. The Holy Spirit was provided to us following his ascension into heaven, and we are saved through faith in him, and we receive the Holy Spirit upon profession of that faith, and baptism in his name.

The Koran denies the divine nature of Jesus, and denies that the Trinity exists, and does not mention the Holy Spirit. When it does list three holy people worshipped by Christianity, the Koran names God, Jesus and Mary, mother of Jesus. Islam teaches a theology that is diametrically opposed to Christianity in every teaching from the Bible. Islam claims that its god is the true God, and that Christians are infidels. The believers of Islam have been led to believe that their god is the same god worshiped by the Christians and Jews. This is not possible according to the teachings of the Bible which the Koran claims to confirm. The Koran also establishes a theology that requires the adherents of its religion to eliminate the followers of any other religion, and promises paradise to those adherents should they lose their lives fighting for their religion.

The God of the Koran places himself above Jesus and claims to be the one and only god; therefore exalting himself above every deity, so that his position is over all. The God of the Bible allows mankind to make a choice whether to revere him, but the God of

PORK, BEEF, CHICKEN AND RIBS

the Koran demands absolute submission and complete allegiance from his followers. Islam demands so much memorization and ritual actions from its adherents that it places the tenants of its teaching in the forefront of their minds on an hourly basis. There are 250 verses in the Koran that young men are required to learn by rote, and to recognize which of these 250 passages they must respond with when the Imam reading the scripture reaches the word "Say." Young men are required to attend an Islamic school called a Madrassa when they reach twelve years of age, where they learn to respond to the "Say" passages from the Koran and other actions required during worship and prayer. Taken as a whole, the religion of Islam is the perfect cult. When you recognize that the God of the Koran is not the Almighty God, you will then recognize that this prophesy from Paul is accurate. The term "deluding influence" describes perfectly the mind control of believers exhibited by Muslims. When it comes to mind that the "God of the Koran," is a being separate from the God of the Bible, many of the apocalyptic prophesies within the Bible are more easily recognized and understood.

I have made the claim that the God of the Koran, is a different being than the God almighty. There is proof of this in the words of the Koran. The God of the Bible, God Almighty, does not change and he cannot lie; therefore, he would not change his plan for salvation as it is written in the Bible, nor deny that Jesus Christ was his only begotten son. When you read what the Koran says, you must remember that the word "God", used in the Koran refers to the God of the Koran, and not to the God of the Bible: but, of course, only one god is professed by the Koran. Now read how the Koran originated.

The prophet Muhammad did not read or write. He received the revelations contained in the Koran from a being he described as the angel Gabriel while he was asleep or in a trance. The historian, Will Durant, in "The Story of Civilization: Part 4," at page 163 tells how Muhammad reported the event to his biographer, Muhammad ibn Ishaq.

> Whilst I was asleep, with a coverlet of silk brocade whereon was some writing, the angel Gabriel appeared to me and said, "Read!" I said, "I do not read." He pressed me with the coverlets so tightly that me thought 'twas death. Then he let me go and said, "Read!"... So I read aloud, and he departed from me at last. And I awoke from my sleep, and it was as though these words were written on my heart. I went forth until, when I was midway on the mountain, I heard a voice from heaven saying, "O Mohammad! Thou art the messenger of Allah, and I am Gabriel." I raised my head towards heaven to see, and lo, Gabriel in the form of a man, with feet set evenly on the rim of the sky, saying, "O Mohammed! Thou art the messenger of Allah, and I am Gabriel."

THE STORY OF CIVILIZATION

Will Durant continues with these words:

> Thereafter he had many similar visions. Often, when they came, he fell to the ground in a convulsion or swoon; perspiration covered his brow; even the camel on which he was sitting felt the excitement, and moved fitfully. Mohammed later attributed his gray hairs to these experiences. When pressed to describe the process of revelation, he answered that the entire text of the Koran existed in heaven, and that one fragment at a time was communicated to him, usually by Gabriel. Asked how he could remember these divine discourses, he explained that the archangel made him repeat every word. Others who were near the Prophet at the time neither saw nor heard the angel.

Now that you are informed as to the way the Koran originated, read other passages which support the purpose of the book, but

PORK, BEEF, CHICKEN AND RIBS

please remember that the god spoken of in the Koran is not the same god known and worshipped by Christians and Jews.

> They say, "God hath begotten children." No! by his glory! he is the self-sufficient. All that is in the heavens and all that is in the earth is his! Have ye warranty for that assertion? What! speak ye of God that which ye know not? SAY: "Verily, they who devise this lie concerning God shall fare ill." A portion have they in this world! Then to us they return! Then make we them to taste the vehement torment, for that they were unbelievers.
>
> Sura 10:69–71 Koran

On two occasions, God in the Bible claims Jesus as his son; at his baptism, and at the transfiguration.

> SAY: "Call upon God (Allah), or call upon the God of Mercy (Arrahman), by whichsoever ye will invoke him: he has most excellent names. And be not loud in their prayer, neither pronounce it too low; but between these follow a middle way." And SAY: "Praise be to God who hath not begotten a son, who hath no partner in the Kingdom, nor any protector on account of weakness." And magnify him by proclaiming his greatness.
>
> Sura 17:110–111 Koran

This denial that God has a son, becomes the source for chants used during daily prayers and other rites required of the followers of Islam.

> They say: "The God of Mercy hath gotten offspring." Now have ye done a monstrous thing! Almost might the very heavens be rent thereat, and the earth cleave asunder, and the mountains fall down in fragments, that they ascribe a son to the God of Mercy, when it beseemeth not the God of Mercy to beget a son! Verily there is none in the heavens

and in the earth but shall approach the God of Mercy as a servant. He hath taken note of them, and numbered them with exact numbering: And each of them shall come to him, on the Day of Resurrection, singly: But love will the God of Mercy vouchsafe to those who believe and do the things that be right. Verily we have made this Koran easy and in thine own tongue, that thou mayest announce glad tidings by it to the God-fearing, and that thou mayest warn the contentious by it. How many generations have we destroyed before them! Canst thou search out one of them? or canst thou hear a whisper from them?

Sura 19:91–98 Koran

Yea, We have brought them the truth; but they are surely liars: God hath not begotten offspring; neither is there any other God with him; else had each god assuredly taken away that which he had created, and some had assuredly uplifted themselves above others! Far from the glory of God, be what they affirm of him! He knoweth alike the unseen and the seen; far be he uplifted above the gods whom they associate with him.

Sura 23:91–92 Koran

The preceding statements give a good indication of the mindset of the author of the Koran. There is a competitiveness in thought that will never understand how Jesus can be one with God. It is in the interest of Islam to renounce anything about Christianity.

Verily, God will not forgive the union of other gods with himself! But other than this he will forgive to whom he pleaseth. And he who uniteth gods with God hath devised a great wickedness.

Sura 4:51 Koran

PORK, BEEF, CHICKEN AND RIBS

> God truly will not forgive the joining of other gods with himself. Other sins he will forgive to whom he will: but he who joineth gods with God, hath erred with far-gone error. They call, besides him, upon mere goddesses! They invoke a rebel Satan!
>
> Sura 4:116–117 Koran

The two mentioned here as Goddess and rebel Satan is Mary and Jesus.

> And of those who say, "We are Christians," have we accepted the covenant. But they too have forgotten a part of what they were taught; wherefore we have stirred up enmity and hatred among them that shall last till the Day of the Resurrection; and in the end will God tell them of their doings. O People of the Scriptures! Now is our Apostle come to you to clear up to you much that ye concealed of those Scriptures, and to pass over many things. Now hath a light and a clear Book come to you from God, by which God will guide him who shall follow after his good pleasure to paths of peace, and will bring them out of the darkness to the light, by his will: and to the straight path will he guide them. (The explanation here is that this Koran is to reveal hidden Bible scripture, and the God of the Koran will lead those who believe this Koran, to paths of peace.) Infidels now are they who say, "Verily, God is the Messiah Ibn Maryam (son of Mary)! SAY: "And who could aught obtain from God, if he chose to destroy the Messiah Ibm Maryam, and his mother, and all who are on the earth together?" For with God is the sovereignty of the heavens and of the earth, and of all that is between them! He createth what he will; and over all things is God potent. (Here the God of the Koran claims the power of the Almighty God.) Say the Jews and Christians, "Sons are we of God and his beloved." *Say*: "Why then doth he chastise you for your sins? Nay! Ye are but a part of the

men whom he hath created!" He will pardon whom he pleaseth, and chastise whom he pleaseth, and with God is the sovereignty of the heavens and of the earth, and of all that is between them, and unto him shall all things return.

Sura 5:17–21 Koran

It is not for the Prophet of the faithful to pray for the forgiveness of those, even though they be of kin, who associate other beings with God, after it hath been made clear to them that they are to be inmates of Hell.

Sura 9:114 Koran

Of old gave we Moses the Book, and they fell to variance about if. If a decree of respite had not gone forth from thy Lord, there had surely been a decision between them. Thy people also are in suspicious doubts about the Koran. And truly thy Lord will repay every one according to their works! For he is well aware of what they do.

Sura 11:112–113 Koran

Note: Here the Koran makes works the basis of a divine reward.

You can see in these statements from the Koran that the basis of Christianity is repudiated and the divinity of Jesus Christ is rejected. There are many other statements in the Koran that teaches beliefs opposite what is taught in the Bible. It is necessary for the reader to reprogram their definition of some words, because the meanings applied in the Koran are different from the meanings we normally apply to them. The word "God," when appearing in the Koran is referring to the God of the Koran, who claims to be the one and only "God." The word "god," refers to any other god other than the God of the Koran. The word "believer," refers to one who believes what the Koran teaches, and accepts the "God of the Koran" as his God. The word does not equate to the word "believer" as used by Christians. The words, "the faithful," are used and at times interchangeable with "believer." The word "infidel," is used to describe anyone who does not believe in the Koran, and the word usually refers to Christians.

While studying the history of Islam, it became obvious that the lack of available Bible scripture, was a key component that aided the initiation of this new religion. This was the result of the famine for the Word of God told about by Amos (Amos 8:11–12 NASB). Bible scripture that was available was probably polluted by the influence of the Nestorian sect which denied that Jesus was divine. The Christian church had become politicized, and Europe was in the throes of depression and the dark ages. There was no effective Christian involvement to counter the rise of Islam, and it spread throughout Arabia during Mohammad's lifetime.

Since early 2002 I have studied Islam and have read through the Koran about ten times, and this resource has contributed to my understanding of the Bible and the prophesies contained within it. The character of God which is expressed with clarity in the Bible makes it impossible for him to be the same god expressed in the Koran. I want to prove this beyond any doubt by scriptural comparisons from the Bible and the Koran. The Koran teaches a theology that conflicts with the Bible, and the words from its pages prove that the "God" of the Koran is separate from the God of the Bible. The Apostle Paul prophesied in 2 Thessalonians 2:1–12 of an apostasy which must occur prior to the return of Christ. This prophesy of an apostasy is fulfilled by the Koran.

Webster's dictionary gives two definitions for the word "apostasy:" 1) renunciation of a religious faith; and 2) abandonment of a previous loyalty. The King James Version of the Bible apparently used the secondary definition by use of the term, "a falling away," where NASB interprets correctly, in my opinion, using the primary definition. The Koran meets the primary definition, and is a renunciation of the Christian religion;

thus, fulfilling Paul's prophesy exactly. When you understand the content of the Koran, you will know this.

The Koran, which I study is the Ballantine Books Edition of April 1993, and is based on the original English translation by J. M. Rodwell, and bears the identification of ISBN 0-8041-1125-1. I enter this information, so that anyone may compare what I write with the book whence it came. I have no formal theological training and have not received any outside instruction on the Koran except for those references used in this presentation. My intent is for what is written in the book to form your opinion as it has formed mine. I began to study the Koran about the time of the attack on the World Trade Center in New York and the Pentagon in the nation's capital. I have read it through about ten times and recorded points of interest in my notes. I have studied closely those parts of the Koran, which I quote here, and believe them important to the understanding of the Muslim way of thinking. I want to present how Islam conflicts with Christianity and show with the words from the Koran that the God of the Koran is a different being than the God of the Bible.

In order to understand the Koran, one must realize that the word "God" does not equate to the same word "God" that is used in the Bible. This is not due to error in translation but to a difference in theology. In the Koran the word "believer" does not equate to a believer in the God of the Bible, but one who accepts Muhammad as a prophet from the God of the Koran and the writings of Muhammad as the word of a true God. The believer then has accepted Islam as their religious belief. It is truly important to understand that the word "believer" does not mean a believer in the God of the Bible. It is also important to know that, "Those who add other gods to God," is the Koran's way of describing Christians. It was difficult for me to understand the intended meaning of Muhammad's writings until I learned these definitions. The recognition of the true meaning of the Koran is greatly enhanced when the proper meaning is applied to the words.

The Koran does not follow a time line or a logical progression of ideas, and it is difficult at times to catch the change in ideas. There seems to be a change in the attitude of the author after his victory over the Meccans, by a more demanding composition. He also takes on a position of being alongside God and uses "we" when making statements attributed to his God. It is recorded that Muhammad did not read or write, and that he dictated the Koran to one of his followers, who wrote the book. Muhammad had to possess an exceptional memory in order to dictate the large amount of scripture contained in the Koran. It seems inconceivable, that with such a memory capacity, that he did not read.

The book of Islam, the Koran, is a complete renunciation of Christianity. Islam teaches an opposite religion from Christianity and demands complete allegiance from its believers. Islam controls the mind of the believer to the extent that the term "brainwashing" is descriptive of the resulting inability of the believer to think logically, or to accept factual data inconsistent with the Islamic model. In Second Thessalonians 2:11, Apostle Paul says that God will send upon them a deluding influence. The mind control exerted by Islam is certainly deluding. Islam is the force perpetrating the apostasy told about by Paul. The purpose of the Koran is given at the start of Sura 18, so read this passage very carefully. From it, I have added explanatory notes in parenthesis.

> praise be to God, who hath sent down the Book (the Koran) to his servant, and hath not made it tortuous but direct; that it may warn of a grievous woe from him, and announce to the faithful who do the things that are right, that a goodly reward, wherein they shall abide forever, awaiteth them; And that it may warn those who say, "God hath begotten a son." No knowledge of this have either

they or their fathers! A grievous saying to come out of their mouths! They speak no other than a lie! And haply, if they believe not in this new revelation (This Koran), thou wilt slay thyself, on their very footsteps, out of vexation. Verily, we (The God of the Koran and Muhammad acting in unison) have made all that is on earth as its adornment, that we might make trial who among mankind would excel in works: (Note that Muhammad makes works the factor to determine a man's relationship with his God of the Koran, rather than faith.) But we are surely about to reduce all that is thereon to dust!

Sura 18:1–7 (Koran)

Did you notice that the God of the Koran and Muhammad take credit for all of creation, with "Verily, We have made all that is on earth as its adornment." Jesus warned of the Muslim inquisition when he said, "an hour is coming for everyone who kills you to think that he is offering service to God. These things they will do because they have not known the Father or me. But these things I have spoken to you, so that when their hour comes, you may remember that I told you of them" (John 16:2–4 NASB). There also seems to be a special place in heaven reserved for the Christian people beheaded by the Muslim believers as a result of the religious competition which Islam directs its believers to kill the infidels and to make Islam the only religion.

> Then I saw thrones and they sat on them, and judgment was given to them. And I saw the souls of those who had been beheaded because of their testimony of Jesus and because of the word of God, and those who had not worshiped the beast or his image, and had not received the mark on their forehead and on their hand.
>
> Revelation 20:4 (NASB)

PORK, BEEF, CHICKEN AND RIBS

This vision which John saw is of a different group than the multitude in white robes told about in Revelation 7: 9–17. The only people taught by their religion to mutilate a human corpse by beheading is the Muslims, and the striking off of the head identifies a religious killing. Jesus was apparently telling of the Muslim religious killings while teaching his disciples and talking with them prior to going to the garden where he was arrested. It is important that those beheaded had not worshiped the beast nor received his mark on their forehead or hand. I interpret the mark of the beast to be a mindset rather than an indelible visual tattoo on the head, or an acceptance of the teachings of the beast for economic reasons, in order to buy and sell, rather than a mark on the hand.

> They will make you outcasts from the synagogue, but an hour is coming for everyone who kills you to think that he is offering service to God. These things they will do because they have not known the Father or me. But these things I have spoken to you, so that when their hour comes, you may remember that I told you of them.
>
> John 16:2–4 (NASB)

This time was fulfilled during the Muslim inquisition, and the practice is a continuing one. The avowed Islamist still thinks that killing a Christian is doing a service to God. The devout Muslim is correct in this assumption when you consider that their God is the God of the Koran, the Antichrist. This prophesy may be related to what the Savior told the Samaritan woman at Jacob's well.

> Woman, believe Me, an hour is coming when neither in this mountain nor in Jerusalem will you worship the Father." Then He continued: "You worship what you do not know; we worship what we know, for salvation is from the Jews. But an hour is coming, and now is, when the true

> worshipers will worship the Father in spirit and truth; for such people the Father seeks to be His worshipers. God is spirit and those who worship him must worship in spirit and truth.
>
> John 4:21 (NASB)

There seems to be a time for everything concerning Jesus to occur as though it was on a schedule, and I have referred to this schedule as a time line because the Scripture uses the words, "there will come a time," or "an hour is coming," and this is significant because an interval of time is being forecast. Daniel 12:7 gives a time interval from his day until the end as "a time, times and half a time," and while we cannot know the interval of time, the verse does indicate that a time line exist. Ecclesiastes 3:1 says that there is a time for everything.

TEACHINGS FROM THE KORAN

Sura 39:24 says, "The best of recitals hath God sent down a book in unison with itself, and teaching by iteration."

A method of teaching—the repetitions are its way of teaching. When I first began to study the Koran, I was surprised to find the large number of repetitions within the narratives. The same story or idea is repeated time after time throughout the book. The explanation of this I found at Sura (or Chapter) 39:24; "The best of recitals hath God sent down—a book in unison with itself, and teaching by iteration."

A method of teaching—the repetitions are its way of teaching. I have heard it said that if you say it often enough, someone will believe. The repetitions, therefore, are an intentional way for the Koran to convince people to believe what it says. It is not an efficient teaching method.

Teaching is usually based on logic, or results of past experiences, or results from scientific research or experiments, or based upon mathematics or other necessary basic knowledge. To admit that such a document as the Koran teaches by iteration (repetition) should be an affront to the author. This statement must have been required by a higher power to be included in the narrative and that is a probability since it is the only unrepeated statement in the entire Koran. The Koran is somewhat difficult to read because of the iterations and the abrupt changes in subject matter. The iterations add considerable length to the book. The first repetitive phrase that I noticed on my first reading was the "gardens beneath which rivers flow," which is the Koran's reference to paradise and descriptive of a place desired by a people accustomed to a nomadic life and desert travel.

> But announce to those who believe and do the things that are right, that for them are gardens 'neath which the rivers flow! So oft as they are fed therefrom with fruit for sustenance, they shall say, 'this same was our sustenance of old,' And they shall have its like given to them. Therein shall they have wives of perfect purity, and therein shall they abide forever.
>
> Sura 2:23 (Koran)

I have recorded thirty-eight similar phrases throughout the book; and there is also a Chapter (called Sura in the Koran) titled "Heaven" that gives more details. The Muslim heaven is much like the life of the rich here on earth, with the addition of dark-eyed virgins, and they are always virgins and many in number. The heaven that is described in the Koran is based on being like this life as a perpetual young man with unlimited sexual capacity and opportunity. The heaven that my God tells about is described as pleasure forevermore (Ps. 16:11 NASB), and says that the heavenly existence is so satisfying that this life will never be remembered or come to mind (Isa. 65:17 NASB). The Old Testament scripture records a case of the prophet Samuel being recalled from the dead, and his displeasure was expressed by what he said: "Why have you disturbed me by bringing me up?" (1 Sam. 28:15, NASB) Samuel would have rather stayed where he was.

I began to record the iterations as I would read through the Koran, and the most repetitive phrase that I found was statements used to promote itself. There are about 150 repetitions which are to convince the reader that it is to be trusted as sent down from God. These are fairly evenly scattered throughout the book with somewhat more occurring in the early chapters. One of these self promoting phrases gives the purpose for the book, but let me warn you that words you are familiar with and understand in the Biblical context have a different meaning when used in the Koran. The word "God" refers to the God of the Koran and not the God of the Bible; and "infidel" is one who does not believe the Koran and the word "Christian" can be interchanged with "infidel." A 'believer' is one who believes the Koran, and 'one who does things that are right' is one who practices Islam and follows the teachings of the Koran. Read again that self-promoting phrase which I surmise to be the purpose for the Koran.

> praise be to God, who hath sent down the Book (the Koran) to his servant, and hath not made it tortuous but direct; that it may warn of a grievous woe from him, and announce to the faithful who do the things that are right, that a goodly reward, wherein they shall abide forever, awaiteth them; And that it may warn those who say, "God hath begotten a son." No knowledge of this have either they or their fathers! A grievous saying to come out of their mouths! They speak no other than a lie! And haply, if they believe not in this new revelation (This Koran), thou wilt slay thyself, on their very footsteps, out of vexation. Verily we (The God of the Koran and Muhammad acting in unison) have made all that is on earth as its adornment, that we might make trial who among mankind would excel in works: (Note that Muhammad makes works the

factor to determine a man's relationship with his God of the Koran, rather than faith.) But we are surely about to reduce all that is thereon to dust!

Sura 18:1–7 (Koran)

The statements designed to promote the Koran are numerous; so I have selected at random the following examples for you to read. Some of them are long because the line of thought being expressed, continues through the entire example. I have added comments in italics and at the end of each example.

> And we sent to you an apostle from among yourselves to rehearse our signs unto you, and to purify you, and to instruct you in "the Book," and in the wisdom, and to teach you that which ye knew not. Therefore, remember me; I will remember you; and give me thanks and be not ungrateful. O ye who believe! Seek help with patience and with prayer for God is with the patient. And say not of those who are slain on God's path that they are dead; nay, they are living! But ye understand not.
>
> Sura 2:146–149 (Koran)

The sayings, "to teach what ye knew not" and "but Ye understand not," is common in the Koran and appears to take a superior or teaching position. This example also supports the teaching that the Muslim killed in service to their God, is alive in Paradise.

> In truth hath he sent down to thee "the Book," which confirmeth those which precede it; for he had sent down the law, and the Evangel aforetime, as man's guidance; and now hath he sent down the "Illumination." (Furkan.) Verily for those who believe not in the signs of God, is a severe chastisement! And God is mighty, the avenger!
>
> Sura 3:2–3 (Koran)

When mention of the Book is made, it is usually followed by the statement that it confirms previous scripture.

> And now have we brought them the Book: with knowledge have we explained it; a guidance and a mercy to them that believe. What have they to wait for now but its interpretation? When its interpretation shall come, they who aforetime were oblivious of it shall say, "The Prophets of our Lord did indeed bring the truth; shall we have any intercessor to intercede for us? or could we not be sent back? then would we act otherwise than we have acted." But they have ruined themselves; and the deities of their own devising have fled from them! Your Lord is God, who in six days created the heavens and the earth, and then mounted the throne: He throweth the veil of night over the day: it pursueth it swiftly: and he created the sun and the moon and the stars, subjected to laws by his behest; Is not all creation and its empire his? Blessed be God the Lord of the worlds!
>
> Sura 7:50–52 (Koran)

The night following day and nature in general is the Koran's argument for the reader to recognize God and similar iterations appear about thirty times in the book. The God of the Koran is referred to as God or Lord of the Worlds about thirty times.

> When thou readest the Koran, have recourse to God for help against Satan the stoned, for no power hath he over those who believe, and put their trust in their Lord, but only hath he power over those who turn away from God, and join other deities with him.
>
> Sura 16:100–102 (Koran)

Those who join other deities with God are Christians.

PORK, BEEF, CHICKEN AND RIBS

Verily they who recite the Book of God, and observe prayer, and give alms in public and in private from what we have bestowed upon them, may hope for a merchandise that shall not perish: God will certainly pay them their due wages, and of his bounty increase them: for he is gracious, grateful.

Sura 35:26–27 (Koran)

HA. MIM. This Book is sent down from God, the mighty, the wise! Assuredly in the heavens and the earth are signs for those who believe: And in your own creation, and in the beasts which are scattered abroad are signs to the firm in faith; And in the succession of night and day, and in the supply which God sendeth down from the heaven whereby he giveth life to the earth when dead, and in the change of the winds, are signs for a people of discernment. Such are the signs of God: with truth do we recite them to thee. But in what teaching will they believe, if they reject God and his signs? Woe to every lying sinner, who heareth the signs of God, recited to him, and then as though he heard them not, persisteth in proud disdain! Apprise him of an afflictive punishment. And when he becometh acquainted with any of our signs he turneth them into ridicule. These! A shameful punishment for them! Hell is behind them! And neither their gains nor the lords whom they have adopted beside God shall avail them in the least; and theirs, a great punishment! This is "Guidance:" And for those who disbelieve the signs of their Lord is the punishment of an afflictive torment.

Sura 45:1–11 (Koran)

Notice that believers are "people of discernment." Lords whom they have adopted besides God, refers to Jesus and the Holy Spirit which Christians name as the Triune God.

You have just read six examples of the arguments put forth in the Koran designed to convince readers that the book is sent from God. There are about 144 other examples that are similar. These repetitions make up a considerable portion of the book, and I estimate that at least a tenth of the book is devoted to these arguments. When you teach by iteration there are many words wasted. Muhammad makes a statement that seems to show his exasperation towards people who will not accept his Koran at Sura 29:50 he writes, "is it not enough for them that we have sent down to thee the Book to be recited to them?" When you read "We," in the Koran it is the Prophet Muhammad and the God of the Koran acting in unison.

The second most repetitive phrase in the Koran, is the admonition for "adding gods to God," and I have recorded 117 instances of that admonition. Since the intent of the Koran is to teach by iteration; and the most repetitive phrase dealing with subject matter is this admonition against Christian belief in the Trinity, then I surmise that the thrust of the book is to oppose Christianity. The Koran in its entirety verifies this evaluation. The prohibition against "adding gods to God," first registered in my mind as those pagans who believed in many gods. It was difficult to conceive that Christ and the Holy Spirit would be considered additional gods. Any question of who is being described by the "adding gods to God" saying is cleared up by the Koran itself.

> Infidels now are they who say, "God is the Messiah, son of Mary;" for the Messiah said,"O children of Israel! Worship God, my Lord and your Lord." Whoever shall join other gods with God, God shall forbid him the garden, and his abode shall be the fire; and the wicked shall have no helpers. They surely are infidels who say, "God is the third of three:" for there is no God but one God: and if they refrain not from what they say, a grievous chastisement shall light on such of them as are infidels. Will they not, therefore, be turned unto God, and ask pardon of him? Since God is forgiving, merciful! The Messiah, son of

PORK, BEEF, CHICKEN AND RIBS

> Mary, is but an apostle; other apostles have flourished before him; and his mother was a just person: they both ate food. Behold! how we make clear to them the signs! then behold how they turn aside!
>
> Sura 5:76–79 (Koran)

Notice that the quote attributed to the messiah; "O children of Israel, worship God, My lord and your Lord," appears to be quite simple and acceptable to almost any readers; however, if you do not read the punctuation, the entire passage seems to be a quote from the Messiah. By quoting Jesus, Muhammad effectively claims his support. Christ made a statement similar to this quote when he said to the devil during his time of temptation; "It is written, 'you shall worship the Lord your God and serve only him.'" Jesus has not made the statement attributed to him here in the Koran; but notice, when read for others to hear, the quote ascribed to Jesus is extended to include additional narrative supporting Islam. The writing in the Koran is deceptive, and this is a good example of that deception, as is the following five verses. This passage makes it clear that the Koran considers Christians to be infidels, and that it is Christians professing the Trinity that are being referred to by the "adding gods to God" statements. Since the iterations are for teaching then it is obvious that the primary intent of the Koran is anti-Christian teaching since this iteration is the most prevalent. The practice of misquoting scripture from the Bible, and then supporting that false statement with the theology of Islam, is prevalent throughout the Koran.

The prohibition against "adding gods to God," which by definition of the Koran, is what Christians do by professing belief in a Triune God: God the Father, God the Son, and God the Holy Spirit. The Koran has absolutely no negative statement about the Holy Spirit and does not visualize a similar being in the faith it professes, unless the Apostle would be considered holding that position. A more accurate description of the position assumed by Muhammad is a position in Islam, equal to that of Jesus Christ in the Christian religion. When making the statement to tell the necessary requirements for a "believer," the Koran usually list: 1. believe in God and his Apostle 2. and give alms, and 3. perform prayer. When I recall what Jesus said that blasphemy against the Holy Spirit is unforgivable; It brings an inkling that the author of the Koran knows this. This theory supports the statement from Mohammad that the whole of the Koran existed in Heaven before it was given to him by the angel Gabriel. Here is what Jesus said about blasphemy against the Holy Spirit:

> Truly I say to you, all sins shall be forgiven the sons of men, and whatever blasphemies they utter; but whoever blasphemes against the Holy Spirit never has forgiveness, but is guilty of an eternal sin.
>
> Mark 3:28–29 (NASB)

The Koran makes the claim sixty-two times that it confirms previous scripture and at Sura 46:11 the previous scripture is called the Book of Moses and the Pentateuch; however, that scripture quoted in the Koran is not from any authentic Hebrew scripture. Sura 137 titled "The Most High", refers to the books of Abraham and Moses as being the books of old. Muhammad's re-creation of the Bible stories from our Old Testament is always different from the Bible. The author of the Koran does not want to convey true Biblical scripture because that would endanger his cause. The stories from the Bible that are written into the Koran, use the same names used in the Bible, but the doctrine is omitted. These stories from the previous scripture make up about half of the total writings in the Koran. It is an error to assume that the scripture confirmed by the Koran is true scripture from the Bible. There is not an accurate statement from the Bible written into the Koran. As I study the

PORK, BEEF, CHICKEN AND RIBS

Biblical scripture which is used in the Koran, I have the distinct feeling that the writer is mocking or ridiculing the scripture. The errors are too glaring to be attributed to just error in translation and to me this indicates an intent to deceive. It is my opinion that the author of the Koran is fabricating similar stories, and claiming them to be from the Bible, which will provide the Muslim with deceptive scripture and prevent any desire to learn additional scripture from the true source. This may be considered a means of mind control that will keep the Muslim from learning true scripture. It was while copying parts of the Koran considered to be previous scripture for readers of this treatise, that I began to see the nature of the writing as ridiculing or mocking the original scriptures. This opinion came while copying the Koran's account of Moses on Mt. Sinai with God from Exodus 33:20–23, which is as quoted below. The stories quoted as scripture are changed in character to be different not only in moral quality, but ridiculous in content from the Bible.

> And we appointed a meeting with Moses for thirty nights, which we completed with ten other nights, so that his whole time with his Lord amounted to forty nights. Then said Moses to his brother Aaron, "Take thou my place among my people and act rightly, and follow not the way of the corrupt doers." And when Moses came at our set time and his Lord spake with him, he said, "O Lord, shew thyself to me, that I may look upon Thee." He said, "Thou shalt not see me; but look toward the mount, and if it abide firm in its place, then shalt thou see me." and when God manifested himself to the mountain he turned it to dust! and Moses fell in a swoon.
>
> Sura 7:138–140 (Koran)

There is not an accurate quote from the Bible, in the Koran; and I repeat, there is not an accurate quote from the Bible, in the Koran. Every quotation of previous scripture is perverted to serve the needs of the author to promote a false impression of the Bible. This is the most significant conclusion to come from my study of the Koran, and this needs to be greatly stressed to people seeking the truth. The majority of the content of the Koran is involved with previous scripture, or stories said to be previous scripture and involving the same named characters which are used in the Bible stories. The quantity of this perverted testimony is difficult to comprehend, but it makes up the majority of the content of the Koran. Over half of the content of the Koran falls into this category of writing by either quoting previous scripture or discussing previous scripture. The bulk of the writing is best described with words like; absurd, fabricated, incongruous, mocking, false or inaccurate.

The Koran urges conflict with the infidels. "He (the God of the Koran) it is who hath sent his Apostle with the guidance and a religion of the truth, that he may make it victorious over every other religion, albeit they who assign partners to God be averse from it" (Sura 9:33). Who are the people who assign partners to God? They are the people who believe the teachings of the Apostle Paul that Jesus was the Messiah, the only begotten Son of God, born of the virgin Mary, and that he was crucified for our salvation and resurrected from the dead, and now sits at the right hand of God the father in Heaven; they are Christians. The obvious conflict between the teachings of the Koran and the teachings of the Bible, indicates that the God of the Koran is a different person from the God of the Bible. Sura CIX (109) seems to accurately depict the situation. It is titled Unbelievers. Remember that unbelievers in this context are Christians. "*Say: O ye Unbelievers!* I worship not that which ye worship, and ye do not worship that which I worship; I shall never worship that which ye worship, Neither will ye worship that which I worship. To you be your religion; to me my religion."

The resurrection is discussed in the Koran about fifty times and the iterations vary from a few words of warning that the judgment is coming to a full description of how an offense may be settled at the resurrection. I mention the number of iterations so that

PORK, BEEF, CHICKEN AND RIBS

you will have knowledge of the quantity of duplication you will experience reading the full book. I hope to provide here the major teachings contained in the Koran without the iterations, so you can gain insight into the belief of the author, without reading the entire book. It is necessary however, to read a great many quotes from the Koran. In order for you to verify what I write, the Sura number and verse will precede each quote. If the reader already knows the Koran, then a quick scan is all that should be necessary. It is the teaching of the Koran that the God of the Koran will be the judge which will determine who goes where on the last day. This teaching is different from the Bible which is normal for the teachings of Islam. The Koran confirms the resurrection but does not confirm the procedural provisions associated with it. While the concept of the resurrection stems from the Bible and the reports are relatively accurate in the Koran pertaining to the event; the concept of who will be subject to judgment and who be the deciding judge is convoluted in the Koran compared to the Bible or vice versa. The Bible teaches that Christians will proceed with Christ to heaven, and their attendance at the judgment waived, because of their faith in Jesus; while the Koran teaches that they are already condemned to the Fire. The Koran teaches that Muslim martyrs will proceed directly to paradise as a reward for fighting and losing their life while fighting for the God of the Koran.

The creation of man is described about fifteen times and here is a good example of that passage.

> Now of fine clay have we created man: Then we placed him, a moist germ, in a safe abode; then made we the moist germ a clot of blood: then made the clotted blood into a piece of flesh; then made the piece of flesh into bones: and we clothed the bones with flesh: then brought forth man of yet another make—Blessed therefore be God, the most excellent of makers—
>
> Sura 23:12–15 (Koran)

Very noticeable by its omission from the Exodus story, is the miracle of the Passover, the tenth and final miracle, and the most widely known because of the annual celebration by the Jews of the Passover. The story of Moses and Pharaoh is partially told, or referenced, about sixteen times in the Koran without mention of the passover and numbering the miracles at *nine*. Muhammad may never have learned about the Passover since he did not read and the Nestorian sect was probably his teachers. The Nestorian monk Bihara is credited with recognizing the twelve-year-old Muhammad as a prophet when he first traveled to Syria with his uncle Abu Talib. The Nestorians were adamant that Jesus was only human, not divine.

John the Baptist alludes to the divine nature of Christ through his proclamation when he said to his disciples following the baptism of Jesus, "Behold the lamb of God." The night that an angel of God took the life of the first born of each household in Egypt, the blood of the Passover (sacrificial) lamb placed on the two doorpost and lintel of the Israeli homes, had caused the angel of death to pass over those homes so marked. John the Baptist was referencing the Passover lamb in his statement following the baptism of Jesus.

The tenth plague which God brought upon the Egyptians through Moses, the Passover, that the Koran ignores is covered in the Bible in Exodus Chapter 12. Here is the most complete of the Koran's stories about the miracles performed against Egypt through Moses:

> We sent Moses with our signs to Pharaoh and his nobles, who acted unjustly in their regard, But see what was the end of the corrupt doers! And Moses said, "O Pharaoh! verily I am an apostle from the Lord of the worlds. Nothing but truth is it right for me to speak of God. Now am I come to you from your Lord with a proof of my mission; send away, therefore, the children of Israel with me." He said "If thou comest with a sign, shew it if thou art a man of truth." So he

PORK, BEEF, CHICKEN AND RIBS

> threw down his rod, and lo! It distinctly became a serpent. Then drew he forth his hand, and lo! It was white to the beholders. The nobles of Pharaoh's people said, "Verily, this is an expert enchanter: Fain would he expel you from your land: what then do ye order to be done?" They said, "Put him and his brother off awhile, and send round men to your cities who shall muster and bring to thee every skilled enchanter." And the enchanters came to Pharaoh. Said they, "Shall we surely be rewarded if we prevail?" He said, "Yes; and ye certainly shall be near my person." They said, "O Moses! Either cast thou down thy rod first, or we will cast down ours." He said, "Cast ye down." And when they had cast them down they enchanted the people's eyes, and made them afraid; for they had displayed a great enchantment. Then spake we unto Moses, "Throw down thy rod;" and lo! It devoured their lying wonders. So the truth was made strong, and that which they had wrought proved vain: And they were vanquished on the spot, and drew back humiliated. But the other enchanters prostrated themselves adoring: said they, "We believe on the Lord of the worlds, the Lord of Moses and Aaron." Said Pharaoh, "Have ye believed on him, ere I have given you leave? This truly is a plot which ye have plotted in this my city, in order to drive out its people. But ye shall see in the end what shall happen. I will surely cut off your hands and feet on opposite sides then will I have you all crucified. They said, "Verily, to our Lord do we return; And thou takest vengeance on us only because we have believed on the signs of our Lord when they came to us. Lord! Pour out constancy upon us and cause us to die Muslims."
>
> Sura 7:101–123 (Koran)

Notice how the Islamic teachings enter into the narrative. The story continues.

> Then said the chiefs of Pharaoh's people, "wilt thou let Moses and his people go to spread disorders in our land,

and desert thee and thy gods?" He said, "We will cause their male children to be slain and preserve their females alive: and verily we shall be masters over them." "We have been oppressed," they said, "before thou camest to us, and since thou hast been with us:" "Perhaps," said he, "your Lord will destroy your enemy, and will make you his successors in the land, and he will see how ye will act therein." Already had we chastised the people of Pharaoh with dearth and scarcity of fruits, that haply they might take warning: And when good fell to their lot they said, "This is our due." But if ill befell them, they regarded Moses and his partisans as (the birds) of evil omen. Yet was not their evil omen from God? But most of them knew it not. And they said, "Whatever sign thou bring us for our enchantment, we will not believe on thee." And we sent upon them the flood and the locust and the kummal (lice) and the frogs and the blood,—clear signs—but they behaved proudly, and were a sinful people. And when any plague fell upon them, they said, "O Moses! pray for us to thy Lord, according to that which he hath covenanted with thee: Truly if thou take off the plague from us, we will surely believe thee, and will surely send the children of Israel with thee." But when we had taken off the plague from them, and the time which God had granted them had expired, behold! They broke their promise. Therefore we took vengeance on them and drowned them in the sea, because they treated our signs as falsehoods and were heedless of them.

Sura 7:124–132 (Koran)

The omission of the more important parts of the story results in a moral and theological emptiness that leaves no important teaching in the Koran's version of the Moses-Pharaoh story. What the author has accomplished is to acknowledge the event as a historical occurrence and to inform the reader of the occurrence without divulging the significance of it. This is the author's way

PORK, BEEF, CHICKEN AND RIBS

of degrading the Bible scriptures and is one of the ways typical to the Koran.

I want to warn the reader again to learn the definition of the words "God", "believer", and "infidel," as they are used in the Koran, because the meanings differ with the definitions we normally apply to these words. The word "God" refers to the God of the Koran and this is my reason for being more precise by referring to my God as "God the Almighty," or "God of the Bible". The word "believer," refers to a person who believes in the God of the Koran, and his apostle, and believes the teachings of the Koran. The word "believer," as used in the Koran, definitely does not refer to a believer in God the Almighty, the God of the Bible, or the God of Abraham, and Isaac, and Jacob who met with Moses at the burning bush. If you are not conscious of this difference in meaning, then you can easily be misled by the Koran. The word "infidel," refers to Christians and to anyone else who does not accept the Koran as Holy. The word most like the meaning of "infidel", as used in the Koran, is the word "Christian." One other word you need to understand is the word "We," which relates to Muhammad, the prophet, and the God of the Koran, acting in unison.

OPPOSING CHRISTIAN AND ISLAMIC THEOLOGY

The purpose of the Koran is to tell the Muslim believer that they will go to Paradise if they follow the teachings of the Koran (do things that are right) and to warn those who say that Jesus is the only begotten Son of God (Christians) that they are wrong and are believing a lie. (Sura 18:1–4) Thus, the theology of Islam is different from the theology taught by the Bible. There are enough opposing teachings to prove that the God of the Koran is a different being from the God of the Bible. The most obvious conflict with Christianity (or opposing theology) put forth in the Koran is the requirement that the Muslim believer take vengeance for his god against nonbelievers or the infidels. The God of the Bible teaches that he is the one to take vengeance, and prohibits the Christian from doing harm to anyone by saying "Vengeance is mine, I will repay" (Deuteronomy 32:35, Romans 12:19). He tells adherents to love their enemies, to feed them if they are hungry, and give them water to drink if they thirst. Then the God of the Bible guarantees that the transgressor will fall in due time, meaning when he decides to take vengeance. He is not a respecter of persons, and treats all people the same, and ask that we do likewise. With him there is no distinction made between rich and poor, free and slave, or male and female; we are all treated the same by the God of the Bible. Remember this and know for certain that you are just as important to the true God, as the priest in the pulpit, or the loan officer at the bank. The God of the Bible prohibited Satan from taking the life of Job when he gave Job into his hand (Job 1:12, NASB). This scripture teaches that Satan does not have the power to take a human life: so therefore, written into the Muslim holy book is the requirement for the Muslim believer to take vengeance against his corporate enemies. Note that in the following passage it is claimed that he (the God of the Koran) could, if he wished, take vengeance himself. This is a false claim.

> When ye encounter the infidels, strike off their heads till ye have made a great slaughter among them, and of the rest make fast the fetters. And afterwards let there either be free dismissals or ransomings till the war hath laid down its burdens. Thus do. Were such the pleasure of God, he could himself take vengeance upon them: but he would rather prove the one of you by the other. And whose fight for the cause of God, their words he will not suffer to miscarry; he will vouchsafe them guidance, and dispose their hearts aright; and he will bring them into the Paradise, of which

PORK, BEEF, CHICKEN AND RIBS

he hath told them. Believers! if ye help God, God will help you, and will set your feet firm: But as for the infidels, let them perish: and their works shall God bring to naught: This—because God is the protector of those who believe, and because the infidels have no protector.

Sura 47:4–12 (Koran)

Remember the definitions because infidels are Christians and the believers are the Muslims.

Early in the reading of the Koran the idea of conflict with the world became obvious by the idea of war, and the Martyr's contract between the God of the Koran and those who fight, insures aggressive response from the believers.

War is prescribed to you: but from this ye are averse. Yet haply ye are averse from a thing, though it be good for you, and haply ye love a thing though it be bad for you. And God knoweth; but ye, ye know not. They will ask thee concerning war in the sacred month. SAY: "To war therein is bad, but to turn aside from the cause of God, and to have no faith in him, and in the Sacred Temple, and to drive out its people, is worse in the sight of God; and civil strife is worse than bloodshed." They will not cease to war against you until they turn you from your religion, if they be able: but whoever of you shall turn from his religion and die an infidel, their works shall be fruitless in this world, and in the next: they shall be consigned to the Fire; therein to abide for aye. But they who believe, and who fly their country, and fight in the cause of God may hope for God's mercy: and God is gracious, merciful.

Sura 2:212–215 (Koran)

And as to those who fled their country for the cause of God, and were afterwards slain, or died, surely with goodly provision will God provide for them! For verily, God! He, surely, is the best of providers! He will assuredly bring them in with an in-bringing that shall please them well: for verily, God is right knowing, gracious.

Sura 22:57–58 (Koran)

Verily, of the faithful hath God bought their persons and their substance, on condition of paradise for them in return: on the path of God shall they fight, and slay, and be slain: a promise for this is pledged in the Law, and in the Evangel (the Pentateuch), and in the Koran—and who more faithful to his engagement than God? Rejoice, therefore, in the contract that ye have contracted: for this shall be the great bliss.

Sura 9:112 (Koran)

Sura 9:112 is referred to as the Martyr's contract.

War was necessary to force the spread of Islam. War was good for Islam because the opposing religious theology of Christianity was eliminated in their area of influence. War or acts of war are the subject of about fifteen narratives in the Koran. Unlike the Koran, a promise to take those killed in war to heaven is not made in the Pentateuch.

Beheading is indicative of a religious killing by a Muslim, because it is prescribed here. At Sura 8:12, it is taught to strike off their heads and every fingertip also. At Sura 5:37, it is taught to slay or crucify or cut off alternate hands and feet. There are about fourteen other verses in the Koran that direct the Muslim to slay the infidels, and do not mention a method to employ. Remember when you read from the Koran that an infidel is a Christian, and God is the god of the Koran. There is also a passage at Sura 17:61 to explain why no miracles are being performed with this statement: "Nothing hindered us from sending thee with the power of working miracles, except that the people of old treated them as lies."

Sura 9, titled "Immunity," establishes how the Muslim is to treat those people existing in an area which they come to

PORK, BEEF, CHICKEN AND RIBS

dominate. "Immunity" establishes a four month time period which these people must be given to decide which religion they will follow or either make a treaty (with the Muslims) which includes paying the impost and certifying the agreement at the mosque. These four months are referred to as the "sacred months." If no agreement is made, this is the provision stated in the Koran to be accomplished by the believers:

> And when the sacred months are passed, kill those who join other gods with God wherever ye shall find them: and seize them; besiege them, and lay wait for them with every kind of ambush: but if they shall convert, and observe prayer, and pay the obligatory alms, then let them go their way, for God is gracious, merciful.
>
> Sura 9:5 (Koran)

> When ye encounter the infidels, strike off their heads until ye have made a great slaughter among them, and of the rest make fast the fetters.
>
> Sura 47:4 (Koran)

During the Muslim inquisition when Yemen was converted, the Jews there made a treaty with the caliph and lived in peace with the Muslims until the nation of Israel was reformed by the United Nations after World War II. Now contrast this teaching with what Jesus taught: "But I say to you, love your enemies and do good to those who hate you" (Matthew 5:44, NASB). There was a recent article in our local newspaper, by a well-educated Muslim who professed that Islam was a religion of peace. If the teachings of the Koran are followed then Islam is peaceful only when everyone converts to Islam, for its teaching is to slay the infidel after the sacred months (the four months of immunity). This feature of the Koran, when implemented, is referred to as "genocide" or "ethnic cleansing." When I realized that the Koran considers a Christian to be an infidel, it became clear that Islam is specifically designed to oppose Christianity. Throughout the Koran I sense an atmosphere of competition that exceeds logical religious preference; and in fact, no preference is permitted by the Koran, outside of the treaty with the Caliph made within the sacred months. Those who are deemed "infidels," have three options to save themselves within the "sacred time;" they can leave the area, convert to Islam, or make the "sacred treaty."

Another major difference between Islam and Christianity is the treatment of women. The Koran teaches the Muslim believer to consider a woman as less important than a man and look upon the woman as a possession of a man. The God of the Bible considers man and woman to be equal, and designed to complement each other. The Bible teaches that marriage is joining one man and one woman together. The true God states that a man and a woman when joined in holy matrimony, become one. Hebrews 13:4 states: "Marriage is to be held in honor among all, and the marriage bed is to be undefiled (do not corrupt the purity or perfection of the sexual relationship between husband and wife); for fornicators and adulterers God will judge." God loved Jacob but hated his twin brother Esau. Esau became a polygamist which is a practice hated by the true God. Paul, in his writing to Timothy reiterates the warning of the apostasy and his description accurately fits the Islamist.

> But the Spirit explicitly says that in the later times, some will fall away from the faith, paying attention to deceitful spirits and doctrines of demons, by means of the hypocrisy of liars seared in their own conscience as with a branding iron, men who forbid marriage and advocate abstaining from foods which God has created to be gratefully shared in by those who believe and know the truth. For everything created by God is good, and nothing is to be rejected if it is received with gratitude.
>
> 1 Timothy 4:1–4 (NASB)

PORK, BEEF, CHICKEN AND RIBS

The Greek word, "koluo" was translated here as, "forbid." A better translation for, "koluo," would be "interfere with," for the primary meaning of the word is "to hinder." Islam does not forbid marriage, but by promoting polygamy, it does hinder marriage. Islam does forbid the eating of pork and drinking of alcoholic beverages. I am impressed by the way Paul"s words "seared in their own consciences as with a branding iron," because that description fits the mindset of the devout Muslim.

Another conflict with Christianity perpetrated by the author of the Koran is the rule of Takiyya, or deception (pronounced tark-e-ya). The teaching is that if a person will be endangered or belittled in revealing their true belief in Islam, then they may deny their Muslim belief with permission from the god of the Koran, if their heart remains committed to Islam. This is lying with approval from their God. The Christian God does not approve of a lie in any form, and makes the truth a major requirement for the Christian believer. One of the Ten Commandments states that you must not bear false witness. A false witness will pervert justice, and the true God promotes justice for all people without partiality. One of the last warnings in the Bible is Rev. 22:15 which condemns all liars. Christians must not fail to acknowledge Jesus Christ as Lord. The teachings of Jesus in his words can be gleaned in this passage: "Whoever denies me before men, I will also deny him before my father in heaven."

In Joshua 24:27 denying the God of the Bible was prohibited. The marked difference in these teachings requires that the inspiration behind them come from different deities.

> Who so after he has believed in God denieth him if he were forced to it and his heart remains steadfast in the faith shall be guiltless.
>
> Sura 16:108 (Koran)

The God of the Bible does not respect the rich more than he does the poor, nor the strong more than he does the weak, nor the man more than he does the woman. This teaching stems from God giving the law to Moses and was first given in the context of judges making decisions in matters before them. Justice is to be administered to all people in a like manner, and their worldly possessions or their worldly position should not be a factor in determining guilt or innocence. This impartiality of God extends to all human relations, even to the seating of congregants in the temple. According to the teachings of the Koran, men are more important than women and the rich are considered more important than the poor. This is wrong in the eyes of the true God. The teaching from the God of the Bible stems from Moses charge to the judges at Horeb.

> You shall not show partiality in judgment; you shall hear the small and the great alike. You shall not fear man, for the judgment is God's. The case that is too hard for you, you shall bring to me, and I will hear it.
>
> Deuteronomy 1:17 (NASB)

Moses was given this instruction by the God of the Bible while the God of the Koran has different ideas.

> God maketh comparison between a slave the property of his lord, who hath no power over anything, and a free man whom we have ourselves supplied with goodly supplies, and who giveth alms therefrom both in secret and openly. Shall they be held equal? No: praise be to God! But most men know it not. God setteth forth also a comparison between two men, one of whom is dumb from his birth, and hath no power over anything and is a burden to his lord: send him where he will, he cometh not back with success. Shall he and the man who enjoineth what is just, and keepeth in the straight path, be held equal?
>
> Sura 16:77–78 (Koran)

PORK, BEEF, CHICKEN AND RIBS

Men are superior to women on account of the qualities with which God hath gifted the one above the other, and on account of the outlay they make from their substance for them. Virtuous women are obedient, careful, during the husband's absence, because God hath of them been careful. But chide those for whose refractoriness ye have cause to fear, remove them into beds apart, and scourge them: but if they are obedient to you then seek not occasion against them: verily, God is high, great!

Sura 4:38 (Koran)

With regard to your children, God commaneth you to give the male the portion of two females.

Sura 4:12 (Koran)

The God of the Bible is not a respecter of persons and teaches his followers to accept the rich, the poor, and the lame in the same spirit. There is no distinction made in the Bible with regards to women being any less important than a man. Old Testament teaching about death benefits, gave a double portion to the first born son, with all later offsprings treated the same, without gender bias.

I will continue to explore these conflicting traits between the God of the Koran and the God of the Bible with the different ways each foretells prophesy to their adherents. One of the most notable passages in the Bible, describing prophesy comes from Amos. Amos was one of the first recorded prophets after Solomon, and recorded the shortcomings of the Hebrews, and the expressions from God.

> You only have I chosen among all the families of the earth; therefore I will punish you for all your iniquities." Do two men walk together unless they have made an appointment? Does a lion roar in the forest when he has no prey? Does a young lion growl from his den unless he has captured

something? Does a bird fall into a trap on the ground when there is no bait in it? Does a trap spring up from the earth when it captures nothing at all? If a trumpet is blown in a city, will not the people tremble? If a calamity occurs in a city, has not the Lord done it? Surely the Lord does nothing unless he reveals his secret counsel to his servants the prophets. A lion has roared! Who will not fear? The Lord God has spoken! Who can but prophesy?

Amos 3:2–7 (NASB)

Amos is explaining the characteristics of God, that he declares to man what his thoughts are through his prophets, and they have no choice but to let that prophesy be known to everyone who will listen. The God of the Koran has a different outlook, and only wants certain of his apostles to know his prophesy and the Koran does not give the criteria for his choosing who is to know.

> It is not in God to leave the faithful in the state in which they are, until he sever the bad from the good; Nor is God minded to lay open the secret things to you, but God chooseth whom he will of his apostles to know them. Believe, therefore, in God and his apostles: and if ye believe and fear God, a great reward awaiteth you.

Sura 3:173–174 (Koran)

Our Christmas routine is to travel to Naples, Florida where my wife cooks the festive meal for her daughter and her extended family. Her daughter has citrus trees which produce good fruit that they seldom harvest. I take it to be my responsibility to save the fruit from the lawnmower which pleases my son-in-law because the grass cutting is easier. Each year I gather as much fruit as I can utilize and transport back home. The juice from the oranges is magnificent and I section and then freeze the grapefruit.

Our great grandson always wanted to help gather the fruit. One Christmas I had both him and his friend, both six years of age, trying to help me. The boys soon began to throw the spoiled fruit that was on the ground at various targets, and, of course, the more rotten the fruit the more fun the game. As one boy would splash an old orange on a tree, some of the splash may get on the other, and that became the object of the game. After a very successful throw the recipient of the splash retaliated by throwing directly at the other boy. The game became war and the ammunition progressed to good fruits from the trees, and, of course, Grandpa intervened to stop the fun. Retaliation is pleasing to the ego. In order for the ego to be satisfied, the retaliation must feel adequate to overcome the feel of the aggression. Thus, aggression and retaliation increase with each cycle of violence, and this is good reason for God to deny retaliation by the individual. Retaliation is permitted for Muslims by the teachings of the Koran.

JESUS DESCRIBED IN THE KORAN

I want you to read from the Koran what it tells about Jesus, because this will give you more insight into the thoughts of the writer. Notice how Jesus is made into an unnatural, superhuman baby, rather than a natural child.

> And remember when the angels said, "O Mary! verily hath God chosen thee, and purified thee, and chosen thee above the women of the worlds! O Mary! Be devout towards thy Lord, and prostrate thyself, and bow down with those who bow." This is one of the announcements of things unseen by thee: To Thee, O Muhammad! Do we reveal it; for thou wast not with them when they cast lots with reeds which of them should rear Mary; nor wast thou with them when they disputed about it. Remember when the angel said, "O Mary! Verily God announceth to thee the word from

him; his name shall be, Messiah, Jesus, the son of Mary, illustrious in this world, and in the next, and one of those who have near access to God; And he shall speak to men alike when in the cradle and when grown up; and he shall be one of the just." She said, "How, O my Lord! Shall I have a son, when man hath not touched me?" He said, "Thus, God will create what he will; When He decreeth a thing, he only saith, 'Be', and it is." And he will teach him the Book, and the wisdom, and the Law, and theEvangel; and he shall be an apostle to the children of Israel. "Now have I come," he will say, "to you with a sign form your Lord; Out of clay will I make for you, as it were, the figure of a bird; and I will breathe into it, and it shall become, by God's leave, a bird. And I will heal the blind, and the leper; and by God's leave will I quicken the dead; and I will tell you what ye eat, and what ye store up in your houses! Truly in this will be a sign for you, if ye are believers. And I have come to attest the Law which was before me; and to allow you part of that which had been forbidden you; and I come to you with a sign from your Lord: Fear God, then and obey me; of a truth God is my Lord, and your Lord: Therefore worship Him. This is a right way.

Sura 3:37–44 (Koran)

And make mention in the Book, of Mary, when she went apart from her family, eastward, and took a veil to shroud herself from them: and We sent Our spirit to her, and he took before her the form of a perfect man. She said: "I fly for refuge from thee to the God of Mercy! If thou fearest him, begone from me." He said: "I am only a messenger of thy Lord, that I may bestow on thee a holy son." She said: "How shall I have a son, when man hath never touched me? And I am not unchaste." He said: "So shall it be. Thy Lord hath said: 'Easy is this with me;' and: "We will make him a sign to mankind, and a mercy from Us. For it is a thing decreed.' "And she conceived him, and retired with him to a far-off place. And the throes came upon her by

PORK, BEEF, CHICKEN AND RIBS

the trunk of a palm...She said: "Oh, would that I had died ere this, and been a thing forgotten, forgotten quite!" And one cried from below her: "Grieve not thou, thy Lord hath provided a streamlet at thy feet:— And shake the trunk of the palm tree towards thee: it will drop fresh ripe dates upon thee. Eat then and drink, and be of cheerful eye: and shouldst thou see a man, Say,—"Verily, I have vowed abstinence to the God of mercy.— To no one will I speak this day." Then came she with the babe to her people, bearing him. They said, "O Mary! now hast thou done a strange thing! O sister of Aaron! Thy father was not a man of wickedness, nor unchaste thy mother." And she made a sign to them, pointing towards the babe. They said, "How shall we speak with him who is in the cradle, an infant" It said, "Verily, I am the servant of God; he hath given me the Book, and he hath made me a prophet; And he hath made me blessed wherever I may be, and hath enjoined me prayer and almsgiving so long as I shall live; And to be duteous to she that bare me: and he hath not made me proud, depraved. And the peace of God was on me the day I was born and will be the day I shall die, and the day I shall be raised to life." This is Jesus, the son of Mary; this is a statement of the truth concerning which they doubt. It beseemeth not God to begat a son. Glory be to him! when he decreeth a thing, he only saith to it, "Be," and it is.

19:16–36 (Koran)

So, we are told a ridiculous, unbelievable, unnatural, and untrue story about Jesus where he speaks as a newborn babe and breathes life into a clay bird. This distortion of the Biblical story is an example of what the Koran claims to be previous scripture. Then we are told a strange story where Mary took a veil to shroud herself and where the God of the Koran, with his apostle, sent their spirit to her to cause the conception of Jesus. Mary vows not to speak and the babe speaks for her, and little of the story sounds like that written in the gospels of Matthew and Luke, six hundred years earlier. The Bible depicts a natural baby and naturally no speech or action is attributed to Jesus as an infant. The story of the Magi following the star and the location has been omitted. No mention is made of the manger, the shepherds or Herod, that appear in the biblical version. There is a continuity within the Bible version which depicts a normal birth that could have occurred within any family. This continuity is lacking in the Koran. The Koran leaves out all the story leading up to the birth and the flight to Egypt following it. The important prophesy concerning the Messiah is not mentioned, and the Koran turns the birth of Christ into an absurdity. The claim to confirm previous scripture is a false claim; and it is made many, many times in the book. There is more for you to read about Jesus in the Koran.

> And for their unbelief. —and for their having spoken against Mary a grievous calumny, —And for their saying, "Verily we have slain the Messiah, Jesus the son of Mary, and apostle of God." Yet they slew him not, and they crucified him not, but they had only his likeness. And they who differed about him were in doubt concerning him: No sure knowledge had they about him, but they followed only an opinion, and they did not really slay him, but God took him up to Himself. And God is mighty, wise! There shall not be one of the people of the Book but shall believe in him before his death, and in the day of resurrection, he will be a witness against them. For the wickedness of certain Jews, and because they turn many from the way of God, We have forbidden them goodly viands which had been before allowed them. And because they have taken usuary, though they were forbidden it, and have devoured men's substance in frivolity, we have got ready for the infidels among them a grievous torment.
>
> 5:155–159 (Koran)

PORK, BEEF, CHICKEN AND RIBS

The idea that they only had the likeness of Christ at the crucifixion was a Gnostic idea and the adherents were called Docetists. They denied that Christ had ever been man, and that his body was only semblance or dokesis.

> And when God shall say—"O Jesus, son of Mary: hast thou said unto mankind — 'Take me and my mother as two gods, beside God?' "He shall say—"Glory be unto thee! It is not for me to say that which I know to be not the truth; had I said that, verily Thou wouldest have known it: Thou knowest what is in me, but I know not what is in Thee; for Thou well knowest things unseen! I spake not to them aught but that which thou didst bid me—'worship God, my Lord and your Lord;' and I was a witness of their actions while I stayed among them; but since thou hast taken me to thyself, thou hast thyself watched them, and thou art witness of all things; If thou punish them, they are thy servants, and if thou forgive them...thou, verily, art the mighty, the wise!"
>
> Sura 5:116–118 (Koran)

This is the longest speech attributed falsely to Jesus that I have noted. It is of course incorrect for Jesus would never deny himself, nor would he lie.

> O ye people of the Book! Overstep not bounds in your religion; and of God, speak only truth. The Messiah, Jesus, son of Mary, is only an apostle of God, and his word which he conveyed into Mary, and a spirit proceeding from himself. Believe therefore in God and his apostles, and say not, "Three:" (there is a trinity)—Forbear it will be better for you. God is only one God! Far be it from his glory that he should have a son! His, whatever is in the heavens, and whatever is in the earth! And God is a sufficient guardian. The Messiah disdaineth not to be a servant of God, nor do the angels who

are nigh unto him. And whoso disdaineth his service, and is filled with pride, God will gather them to all himself.

Sura 4:169–171 (Koran)

And Mary, the daughter of Imran, who kept her maidenhood, and into whose womb we breathed of our spirit, and who believed in the words of her Lord and his scripture, and was one of the devout.

Sura 56:12 (Koran)

Now you have read most of the passages relating to Jesus as they appear in the Koran. The author of the Koran, always has Jesus deny that he is the Son of God, and of course he is not the son of the God of the Koran. Quotations are attributed to Jesus, which he has not uttered and are supportive of the Koranic teachings that there are "no partners with God."

Christians know that Christ would never deny the Trinity, since he foretold of the coming of the Holy Spirit and is himself a part of the Trinity. It is difficult to keep the God of the Koran in his proper perspective when only the word "God" is used. Notice how the writings seem to gather the support of Mary in the last example while also taking credit for fathering Jesus.

The God of the Bible does not change! This characteristic of God is sure and he tells us of this trait many times throughout the Bible. The God of the Koran wants the Muslim to accept what he has placed into the Koran, as the scriptures of old, in order that they have contempt for the Bible and prevent them from wanting to read the Bible. The God of the Bible cannot be the God of the Koran, because that would require that he change, or lie, and he can do neither. The God of the Koran is another being, different from the God of the Bible. The Koran claims to confirm the scriptures of old but in every example the scripture is misquoted and is usually twisted around to a narrative supportive of Islamic theology. It is obvious to Christians that the God of the Bible would not be a part of the Koran, just because of the failure to recognize the deity of Jesus. Not only does the Koran deny the deity of Jesus but blatantly fabricates false scripture claiming his support for Islam. There is a statement, in the Bible, that Jesus made describing Satan, and this is a good place to have an accurate duplication of previous scripture. Here is Jesus speaking to the Jews claiming Abraham as their father.

> If God were your Father, you would love me, for I proceeded forth and have come from God, for I have not even come on my own initiative, but he sent me. Why do you not understand what I am saying? It is because you cannot hear my word. You are of your father, the devil, and you want to do the desires of your father. He was a murderer from the beginning, and does not stand in the truth because there is no truth in him. Whenever he speaks a lie, he speaks from his own nature, for he is a liar and the father of lies.
>
> John 8:44 (NASB)

RETALIATION

There is good reason to refer to Satan as the Deceiver. There is much more that you should read in the Koran, but you must recognize that the God of the Hebrew scriptures, is not a part of this book. God the Almighty reserves retaliation for himself and commands that we shall not kill. Deuteronomy 32:35 and 41 is his attitude on retaliation, where he says "vengeance is mine, I will repay," and the sixth commandment from Exodus 20:13 is "thou shall not murder." The Koran has much more to say about retaliation, and vengeance is permitted in proportion to the offense, provided that the violence is not done during the pilgrimage or at the mosque. Read what is written about retaliation in the Koran.

O believers! Retaliation for bloodletting is prescribed to you: the free man for the free, and the slave for the slave and the woman for the woman; but he to whom his brother shall make any remission, is to be dealt with equitably; and to him should he pay a fine with liberality. This is a relaxation from your lord and a mercy. For him who after this shall transgress, a sore punishment! But this law of retaliation is your security for life, O men of understanding! To the intent that ye may fear God.

Sura 2:173–175 (Koran)

The sacred month and the sacred precincts are under the safeguard of reprisals: whoever offereth violence to you, offer ye the like violence to him, and fear God, and know that God is with those who fear him.

Sura 2:190 (Koran)

When thy Lord spoke unto the angels, "I will be with you: therefore establish ye the faithful. I will cast a dread into the hearts of the infidels." Strike off their heads then, and strike off from them every fingertip. This, because they have opposed God and his Apostle; and who so shall oppose God and his apostle...Verily, God will be severe in punishment." This for you! Taste it then! And for the infidels is the torture of the Fire! O ye who believe! When ye meet the marshalled host of the infidels, turn not your backs to them: Who so shall turn his back to them on that day, unless he turn aside to fight, or to rally to some other troop, shall incur wrath from God: Hell shall be his abode and wretched the journey thither!

Sura 8:12–16 (Koran)

And whoever in making exact reprisal for injury done him, shall again be wronged, God will assuredly aid him: for God is most merciful, gracious."

Sura 22:59 (Koran)

PORK, BEEF, CHICKEN AND RIBS

When ye encounter infidels, strike off their heads till ye have made a great slaughter among them, and of the rest make fast the fetters. And afterwards let there either be free dismissals or ransomings, till the war hath laid down its burdens. Thus do. Were such the pleasure of God, he could himself take vengeance upon them: but he would rather prove the one of you by the other. And who so fight for the cause of God, their words he will not suffer to miscarry; he will vouchsafe them guidance, and dispose their hearts aright; and he will bring them into paradise, of which he hath told them. Believers! If ye help God, God will help you, and will set your feet firm: But as for the infidels, let them perish: and their works shall God bring to nought: This—because they were averse from the command which God sent down; fruitless, therefore, shall their works become! Have they not journeyed through the land, and seen what hath been the end of those who flourished before them? God brought destruction on them: and the like of this doth await the infidels. This—because God is the protector of those who believe, and because the infidels have no protector.

Sura 47:4–12 (Koran)

O Prophet! Make war on the infidels and hypocrites, and deal rigorously with them. Hell shall be their abode! And wretched the passage to it!

Sura 56:9 (Koran)

You can recognize the difference in the two teachings on retaliation, where one forbids it and the other prescribes vengeance and condones violence. Some passages in the Koran do more than just condone violence but demands it of the believer, against the infidel. It is not a crime under Islamic law for a Muslim to take the life of an infidel; it becomes a duty for the believer.

When a decapitated body is found with the fingers cut off, you can know that the killing was inspired by Islam (Sura 8:12–

16). It is the intent of Islam to become the only religion, or to be victorious over every other religion, and violence is a part of the contest. Notice the statement at Sura 47:5 "Were such the pleasure of God, he could himself take vengeance upon them: but he would rather prove the one of you by the other."

If the God of the Koran is Satan then this is of course a lie, because Satan does not have the power to take the life of a human being. Continue to read the passages relating to violence against the infidels. Remember the meaning of the words "infidel," "God," and "believer," so that you will not misunderstand.

> O believers! Only they who join gods with God are unclean! Let them not, therefore, after this their year, come near the Sacred Temple. And if ye fear want, God, if he pleases, will enrich you of his abundance: for God is knowing, wise. Make war upon such of those to whom the Scriptures have been given as believe not in God, or in the Last Day, and who forbid not that which God and his Apostle have forbidden, and who profess not the profession of the truth, until they pay tribute out of hand, and they be humbled. The Jews say, "Ezra (Ozair) is a son of God," and the Christians say, "the messiah is a son of God." Such the sayings in their mouths! They resemble the saying of the infidels of old! God do battle with them! How they are misguided! They take their teachers and their monks, and the Messiah, son of Mary, for lords besides God, though bidden to worship one God only. There is no God but he! Far from his glory be what they associate with him! Fain would they put out God's light with their mouths: But God only desireth to perfect his light, albeit the infidels abhor it. He, it is who hath sent his Apostle with the guidance and a religion of truth, that he may make it victorious over every other religion, albeit they who assign partners to God be averse from it.
>
> Sura 9:28–33: (Koran)

PORK, BEEF, CHICKEN AND RIBS

Believers! When ye confront a troop, stand firm, and make frequent mention of the name of God, that it may fare well with you. (Sura 8:42) And know ye, that when ye have taken any booty, a fifth part belongeth to God and to the Apostle, and to the near of kin, and to orphans, and to the poor, and to the wayfarer, if ye believe in God, and in that which We have sent down to our servant on the day of the victory, the day of the meeting of the hosts. Over all things is God potent.

Sura 8:47 (Koran)

Verily, of the faithful hath God bought their persons and their substance, on condition of paradise for them in return: on the path of God shall they fight, and slay, and be slain: a promise for this is pledged in the Law, and in the Evangel, and in the Koran—and who more faithful to his engagement than God? Rejoice, therefore, in the contact that ye have contracted: for this shall be the great bliss.

Sura 9:112 (Koran)

Believers! Wage war against such of the infidels as are your neighbors, and let them find you rigorous: and know that God is with those who fear Him.

Sura 9:24 (Koran)

Vengeance, retaliation, strike off their heads, make war against, genocide, ethnic cleansing: these are all used to describe the violence done to the "infidel," by the faithful Muslim. Perhaps we can determine with reasonable accuracy the two and a half million Christians killed in Darfur and southern Sudan in recent years, but it is impossible to estimate the number of those killed by Muslims throughout their expansion in the dark ages.

THE NOAH STORIES

Another way the Koran works to eliminate the true Bible scripture is to fabricate scripture and attach the fabrication to a known event with known people. The Koran's version of the story of Noah is an example of this method. The most brazen use of fabricated scripture is in the Noah stories. The actual story of *Noah and The Ark* begins with God saying to Noah, (Genesis 6:13) "The end of all flesh has come before me; for the earth is filled with violence because of them; and behold, I am about to destroy them with the earth." Noah has no speaking part in the book of Genesis, for the story is only about what God has done. God found the people of the earth unacceptable to him, with the exception of Noah. He decided to destroy the people of the earth and to have Noah rescue his family and breeding pairs of all animals. God then gives Noah the instructions for building the ark and loading it. No statement is recorded that Noah spoke, until long after the flood and after he had a grandson, Canaan, son of Ham; and that speech did not relate to the flood. Noah had become drunk on wine from his vineyard, and Ham had violated his privacy. This is the only statement that Noah uttered that is recorded in the Bible.

> Cursed be Canaan; a servant of servants he shall be to his brothers." "Blessed be the Lord, the God of Shem; and let Canaan be his servant. May God enlarge Japheth, and let him dwell in the tents of Shem; and let Canaan be his servant."
>
> Genesis 9:25–27 (NASB)

Now that you know that Noah had no speaking part until long after the flood; read the fabrications about Noah from the Koran, but remember that the word "God," means the God of the

PORK, BEEF, CHICKEN AND RIBS

Koran and not the God of the Bible. Remember as you read that all of the Noah stories are fabrications.

> Recite to them the history of Noah, when he said to his people, "If, O my people! my abode with you, and my reminding you of the signs of God, be grievous to you, yet in God is my trust; Muster, therefore, your designs and your false gods, and let not your design be carried on by you in the dark: then come to some decision about me, and delay not. And if ye turn your backs on me, yet ask I no reward from you: my reward is with God alone, and I am commanded to be of the Muslims." But they treated him as a liar: therefore we rescued him and those who were with him in the Ark, and we made them to survive the others; and we drowned those who charged our signs with falsehood. See, then, what was the end of these warned ones!
>
> Sura 10:72–74 (Koran)

We sent Noah of old unto his people: —"Verily I come to you a plain admonisher, that ye worship none but God. Verily I fear for you the punishment of a grievous day." Then said the chiefs of his people who believed not, "We see in thee but a man like ourselves; and we see not who have followed thee except our meanest ones of hasty judgment, nor see we any excellence in you above ourselves, nay, we deem you liars."

He said: "O my people! How think you If I am upon a clear revelation from my Lord, who hath bestowed on me mercy from himself to which ye are blind, can we force it on you, if ye are averse from it? And, O my people! I ask you not for riches: my reward is of God alone: and I will not drive away those who believe that they shall meet their Lord:—but I see that ye are an ignorant people. And O my people! Were I to drive them away, who shall help me against God? Will ye not therefore consider? And I tell you not that with me are the treasures of God: nor do I say, 'I know the things unseen;' nor do I say, 'I am an angel;' nor do I say of those whom you eye with scorn, 'No good thing will God bestow on them:'—God best knoweth what is in their minds—for then should I be one of those who act unjustly."

They said: "O Noah! Already hast thou disputed with us, and multiplied disputes with us: Bring then upon us what thou hast threatened, if thou be of those who speak truth." He said, "God will bring it on you at his sole pleasure, and it is not you who can weaken him; nor, if God desire to mislead you, shall my counsel profit you, though I fain would counsel you aright. He is your Lord and unto him shall ye be brought back.

Do they say, "This Koran is of his own devising" Say: "On me be my own guilt, if I have devised it, but I am clear of that where of ye are guilty." And it was revealed unto Noah. "Verily, none of thy people shall believe, save they who have believed already; therefore be not thou grieved at their doings. But build the Ark under our eye and after our revelation: and plead not with me for the evildoers, for they are to be drowned."

So he built the Ark; and whenever the chiefs of his people passed by they laughed him to scorn: said he, "Though ye laugh at us, we truly shall laugh at you, even as ye laugh at us; and in the end ye shall know on whom a punishment shall come that shall shame him, and on whom shall light a lasting punishment."

Thus was it until Our sentence came to pass, and the earth's surface boiled up. We said, "Carry into it one pair of every kind, and thy family, except him on whom sentence hath before been passed, and those who have believed."

But there believed not with him except a few. And he said, "Embark ye therein. In the name of God be its course and its riding at anchor! Truly my Lord is right gracious, merciful." And the Ark moved on with them amid waves like mountains; and Noah called to his son—for he was apart— "Embark with us, O my child! and be not with the unbelievers." He said, "I will betake me to a mountain that

PORK, BEEF, CHICKEN AND RIBS

shall secure me from the water." He said, "None shall be secure this day from the decree of God, save him on whom he shall have mercy." And a wave passed between them, and he was among the drowned.

And it was said, "O earth! swallow up thy water," and "cease, O heaven!" And the water abated, and the decree was fulfilled, and the Ark rested upon Al-Djoudi; and it was said, "Avaunt! ye tribe of the wicked!" And Noah called upon his Lord and said, "O Lord! verily my son is of my family: and thy promise is true, and thou art the most just of judges."

He said, "O Noah! verily, he is not of thy family: in this thou actest not aright. Ask not of me that whereof thou knowest nought: I warn thee that thou become not of the ignorant. He said, "To thee verily, O my Lord, do I repair lest I ask that of thee wherein I have no knowledge: unless thou forgive me and be merciful to me I shall be one of the lost."

It was said to him, "O Noah! Debark with peace from us, and with blessings on thee and on peoples to be born from those who are with thee; but as for other and unbelieving peoples, we will give them their good things in this world, but hereafter shall a grievous punishment light on them from us." This is one of the secret Histories: We reveal it unto thee: neither thou nor thy people knew it ere this: be patient thou: verily, there is a prosperous issue to the God-fearing.

Sura 11:27–51 (Koran)

None of the words attributed to Noah was said. None of these conversations took place, nor did Noah have a son drown in the flood, and there is no secret history with the God of the Bible.

We sent Noah to his people and said to him, "Warn thou thy people ere there come on them an afflictive punishment." He said, "O my people! I come to you a plain-spoken warner: Serve God and fear him and obey me: Your sins will he forgive you, and respite you till the fixed time: for when God's fixed time hath come, it shall not be put back. Would that ye knew this!

Sura 71:1–4 (Koran)

None of this is correct, and was not in previous scripture. Noah was not sent, but was the only family rescued because Noah was righteous. Muhammad is making the same argument using the name of Noah that he made himself, against his own people who would not listen to him. All the writings about Noah in the Koran is fabricated, and designed to promote the Islamic teachings.

Before leaving the Noah writings I want to copy one more example of the story so that the similarity can be seen between the Noah stories which are known fabrications, and stories with other main characters but with the same pattern of expression. The stories always place the main character as a plain warner bringing a theology and a God, and seeking support. Muhammad was criticized for associating with ruffians and this is brought out in the story, with the same refusal to effect any disassociation with them. Then according to the fable, God destroys the people who would not accept the new teaching, and Muhammad claims that this is a sign from his god.

> The people of Noah gain said the apostles, when their brother Noah said to them, "Will ye not fear God? Of a truth am I your faithful apostle; fear God then and obey me. I ask of you no reward for this, for my reward is of the Lord of the Worlds alone: Fear God then and obey me." They said, "Shall we believe on thee when the meanest only are thy followers?" He said, "But I have no knowledge of that they did: To my Lord only must their account be given: would that ye understood this! And I will not thrust

away those who believe, for I am only one charged with plain warnings."

They said, "Now unless thou desist, O Noah, one of the stoned shalt thou surely be." He said, "Lord! my people treat me as a liar: Decide thou therefore a decision between me and them, and rescue me and the faithful who are with me." So we saved him and those who were with him in the fully laden ark, and afterwards we drowned the rest. Herein truly was a sign, but most of them believed not. But thy Lord! —he is mighty, the merciful.

Sura 26:105-121 (Koran)

Muhammad has taken a known tale, the flood, and the known main character, Noah, and fabricated a story which is designed to support Islam. None of the conversations reported, supposing to be previous scripture, ever happened. The fact that the Koran claims to confirm previous scripture when it does not do so is deceiving. Muhammad has attempted to change history with fabrications.

There are still important teachings of the Koran which you must know. The way Islam looks upon women is a major part of the doctrine. Islam does not regard a woman to be as important as a man. This fact is firmly expressed by Asra Q. Nomani in her book "Standing Alone." There is an increasing effort by women to gain a more favorable position within Islam and I suspect that they will have some success. Women will lead the exodus from Islam in future years as opportunities occur for them to safely do so. The following excerpts are related to sexual relations, marriage, and divorce. Some of the Islamic traditions may surprise you and all the excerpts will help you to understand the mindset of the Muslim people.

Sexual relations between close relatives is forbidden in the Koran similar to all laws and religious practice. There are some notable exceptions in the Koran.

> Forbidden to you also are married women except those who are in your hands as slaves: This is the law of God for you. And it is allowed you beside this, to seek out wives by means of your wealth, with modest conduct, and without fornication. And give those with whom ye have cohabited their dowry. This is the law. But it shall be no crime in you to make agreements over and above the law. Verily, God is knowing, wise!
>
> Sura 4:28 (Koran)

This is the provision that allow men to make temporary marriages of convenience with women who are not otherwise committed to a sexual relationship. An example of this arrangement was told about in an article by Nancy Trejos of the Washington Post, January 21, 2007, titled "Enjoyment marriages back in Iraq." According to the article a thirty-four-year-old Shiite sheik, with a pregnant wife who, he said, could not have sex with him, entered into a "mutaa," or enjoyment marriage with an unemployed twenty-four-year-old divorcee. This temporary union is believed by Shiite Muslims to be sanctioned by Islamic law.

One of the basic tenets of Islamic law is that men are more important than women, and this is stated unequivocally in Sura 4:38, and disobedient wives can be legally scourged. A man can have as many wives as he can support, while the woman does not have such an opportunity. The legal position of a woman under Islamic law is similar to that of a child, and it appears that the Koran considers a woman incapable of looking after her own affairs.

> Men are superior to women on account of the qualities with which God hath gifted the one above the other, and on account of the outlay they make from their substance for them. Virtuous women are obedient, careful, during the husband's absence, because God hath of them been

PORK, BEEF, CHICKEN AND RIBS

careful. But chide those for whose refractoriness ye have cause to fear, remove them into beds apart, and scourge them: but if they are obedient to you them seek not occasion against them: verily, God is high, great!

Sura 4:38 (Koran)

of other women who seem good in your eyes, marry but two, or three, or four, and if ye still fear that ye shall not act equitably, then one only; or the slaves whom ye have acquired: this will make justice on your part easier. Give women their dowry freely; but if of themselves they give up aught thereof to you, then enjoy it as convenient, and profitable: And entrust not to the incapable the substance which God hath placed with you for their support; but maintain them therewith, and clothe them, and speak to them with kindly speech.

Sura 4:3–4 (Koran)

And whoever of you is not rich enough to marry free believing women, then let him marry such of your believing maidens as have fallen into your hands as slaves; God well knoweth your faith. Ye are sprung the one from the other. Marry them, then, with the leave of their masters, and give them a fair dower: but let them be chaste and free from fornication, and not entertainers of lovers.

Sura 4:29 (Koran)

And if a wife fear ill usage or aversion on the part of her husband, then shall it be no fault in them if they can agree with mutual agreement, for agreement is best. Men's souls are prone to avarice; but if ye act kindly and fear God, then, verily, your actions are not unnoticed by God!

Sura 4:127 (Koran)

And ye will not have it at all in your power to treat your wives alike, even though you fain would do so; but yield not wholly to disinclination, so that ye leave one of them as it were in suspense; if you come to an understanding, and fear God, then, verily, God is forgiving, merciful; But if they separate, God can compensate both out of his abundance; for God is vast, wise.

Sura 4:128 (Koran)

DIVORCE IN THE KORAN

Divorce is prescribed in the Koran, at the discretion of the husband.

The divorced shall wait the results, until they have had their courses thrice, nor ought they conceal what God hath created in their wombs, if they believe in God and the Last Day; and it will be more just in their husbands to bring them back when in this state, if they desire what is right. And it is for the women to act as they (the husbands) act by them, in all fairness; but the men are a step above them. God is mighty, wise.

Ye may divorce your wives twice: keep them honorably, or put them away with kindness. But it is not allowed you to appropriate to yourselves aught of what ye have given to them, unless both fear that they cannot keep; within the bounds set up by God, And if ye fear that they cannot observe the ordinances of God, no blame shall attach to either of you for what the wife shall herself give for her redemption. These are the bounds of God; Therefore overstep them not: for whoever oversteppeth the bounds of God, they are evil Doers.

When ye divorce women and the time for sending them away has come, either retain them with generosity, or put them away with generosity: but retain them not by constraint so as to be unjust towards them. He who doth so, doth in fact injure himself. And make not the signs of God a jest; but remember God's favor towards you, and the Book and the Wisdom which He hath sent down to you for your warning, and fear God, and know that God's knowledge embraceth everything.

And when ye divorce your wives, and they have waited the prescribed time, hinder them not from marrying their husbands when they have agreed among themselves in an honorable way.

This warning is for him among you who believeth in God and in the Last Day. This is most pure for you, and most decent. God knoweth, but ye know not. Mothers, when divorced, shall give suck to their children two full years, if the father desire that the suckling be completed; and such maintenance and clothing as is fair for them, shall devolve on the father. No person shall be charged beyond his means. A mother shall not be pressed unfairly for her child, or a father for his child: and the same with the father's heir but if they choose to wean the child by consent and by bargain, it shall be no fault in them. And if ye choose to have a nurse for your children, it shall be no fault in you, in case ye pay what ye promised her according to that which is fair. Fear God and know that God seeth what ye do.

Sura 2:228–233 (Koran)

OTHER TEACHINGS

Now you have read most of the significant passages of the Koran. There are a few more passages that are interesting to know, but the end is near. Notice that there is no middle way that is comfortable with Islam, because controversy about the Koran is made obnoxious, abhorrent by its teachings. The Koran demands that all people believe what it teaches is right, or they will automatically become opponents to the other people who do believe, and be known as "Infidels."

> Of a truth they who believe not on God and His apostles, and seek to separate God from His apostles, and say, "Some we believe, and some we believe not," and desire to

take a middle way; These! They are veritable infidels! And for the infidels have we prepared a shameful punishment. And they who believe on God and His apostles, and make no difference between them—these! We will bestow on them their reward at last. God is gracious, merciful!

Sura 4:149–150 (Koran)

This passage gives some of the characteristics of a believer. Other characteristics included in some of the more than thirty iterations which list these characteristics include; "observe prayer, and pay the impost or give alms." Always included is believe in God and his apostles. It is necessary to reiterate here that the God of the Koran is just that: The characteristics of the God of the Koran define a being much different from the God of the Bible.

Two passages of interest appear to be directed at individuals in the Koran. One deals with the Prophet's wives and one with someone who has displeased the Prophet. The God of the Bible, would not have the attitude that is put forth with these passages.

> Why, O Prophet! dost thou hold that to be *Forbidden* which God hath made lawful to thee, from a desire to please thy wives, since God is lenient, merciful? God hath allowed you release from your oaths; and God is your master: and He is Knowing, Wise. When the Prophet told a recent occurrence as a secret to one of his wives, and when she divulged it and God informed him of this, he acquainted her with part and withheld part. And when he had told her of it, she said, "Who told thee this?" He said "The Knowing, the Sage hath told it to me." If ye both be turned to God in penitence, for now have your hearts gone astray…but if ye conspire against the Prophet then know that God is his Protector, and Gabriel, and every just man among the faithful; and the angels are his helpers besides. Haply if he put you both away, his Lord will give him in exchange other wives better than you, Muslims,

PORK, BEEF, CHICKEN AND RIBS

believers, devout, penitent, obedient, observant of fasting, both known of men and virgins.

Sura 56:1–5 (Koran)

The second passage is directed to one who has displeased Muhammad.

Let the hands of ABU LAHAB perish, and let himself perish! His wealth and his gains shall avail him not. Burned shall he be at the fiery flame, and his wife laden with firewood,—On her neck a rope of palm fibre.

Sura 111:1–5 (Koran)

According to Muhammad, the God of the Koran will be the judge on resurrection day, and excludes the possibility of any intercessor.

The day when they shall come forth from their graves, when nought that concerneth them shall be hidden from God. With whom shall be the power supreme on that day? With God, the One, the Almighty. On that day shall every soul be recompensed as it hath deserved: no injustice on that day! Verily, God will be swift to reckon.

Sura 40:16–17 (Koran)

And everything will God decide with truth: but nothing shall those gods whom men call on besides him, decide. Verily God! the hearer, the beholder, he!

Sura 40:21 (Koran)

And quit those who make their religion a sport and a pastime, and whom this present life hath deceived: warn them hereby that every soul will be consigned to doom for its own works: patron or intercessor, besides God, shall it have none: and could it compensate with fullest compensation, it would not be accepted from it. They who for their deeds shall be consigned to doom—for them are draughts of boiling water, and a grievous torment for that they believed not!

Sura 6:69 (Koran)

When the Koran refers to other gods men call on besides God, and patron or intercessor besides God, the reference is to Jesus. This conflicts with the Biblical teachings that all power is given to Christ Jesus to judge the world at the resurrection. It also counters the Christian belief that Jesus was made a sacrifice for the sins of those who believe on him. Christ makes the claim in Matthew 25:31 that he will separate the sheep from the goats when he comes in his glory, on the last day or the day of resurrection. Paul teaches in Second Corinthians 5:10, "For we must all appear before the judgment seat of Christ, so that each one may be recompensed for his deeds in the body, according to what he has done, whether good or bad."

This is another teaching of Islam that contradicts the teaching of Christianity, and there are a few, if any, points of agreement within the two religions. The cardinal sin according to the God of the Koran, is to believe in Jesus Christ as the Son of God. This one trait is adequate proof that he is not the same god as described in the Bible. I have endeavored to show this fact in other ways, and hope that I have succeeded. It is important that all Christians recognize the anti-Christian fervor expressed in the Koran, for this places it in the lap of the devil—the Antichrist—Satan.

SUMMARY

You have read the major teachings from the Koran. There are many words wasted in iterations within the book, which you have evaded, but here is a summary of the iterations. About 150 times throughout the book there are passages seeking the readers' acceptance and accounts for a tenth of the words in the book. I have recorded 117 instances where the people, who add gods to God, are denounced; and in most of these admonitions refer to Christians calling Jesus "Lord".

The third most prevalent iteration, and appearing at least sixty-two times, is the claim to confirm previous scripture, which is a false claim. The Koran intentionally belittles the Bible scripture. There is a demonstration of a huge knowledge of the Bible, but the scriptures quoted are changed to either make them appear ridiculous or cause them to support Koranic teaching. The distorted scripture and the commentary connected with it, make up over half of the words in the Koran.

The Koran's version of *paradise* is described over thirty times, and there are sixteen different entries dedicated to the Koran's version of Moses with the Pharaoh story. Appearing about eight times is a non-Biblical narrative about God telling the angels to bow down and worship Adam, and all did except Eblis (Satan).

> And when We said to the angels, "Prostrate yourselves before Adam:" and they all prostrated them, save Eblis, "What!" said he, "Shall I bow me before him whom thou hast created of clay?" Seest thou this man whom thou hast honoured above me? Verily, if thou respite me till the Day of Resurrection, I will destroy his offspring, except a few." He said, "Begone; but whosoever of them shall follow thee, verily, Hell shall be your recompense; an ample recompense! And entice such of them as thou canst by thy voice; assault them with thy horsemen and thy footmen; be their partner in their riches and in their children, and make them promises: but Satan shall make them only deceitful promises.
>
> Sura 17:63–66 (Koran)

Also duplicated perhaps eight times, the story of Lot at Sodom, usually followed by a narrative on someone named AD and Themoud, and then the story of a she camel, that was hamstrung. The resurrection is mentioned about thirty-two times and referred to as "Judgment Day" a few more times. The only statement that is not repeated that I have noticed is the statement about the Koran teaching by iteration. Only once does this statement appear. The following passage is included here because it claims to be part of the wisdom revealed in the Koran.

> Set not up another god with God, lest you sit thee down disgraced, helpless. Thy Lord hath ordained that ye worship none but him; and, kindness to your parents, whether one or both of them attain to old age with thee: and say not to them, "Fie!" neither reproach them; but speak to them both with respectful speech; and defer humbly to them out of tenderness; and say, "Lord, have compassion on them both, even as they reared me when I was little."
>
> Your Lord well knoweth what is in your souls; he knoweth whether ye be righteous; And gracious is he to those who return to him. And to him who is of kin render his due, and also to the poor and to the wayfarer; yet waste not wastefully, for the wasteful are brethren of the satans, and Satan was ungrateful to his Lord: But if thou turn away from them, while thou thyself seekest boons from thy Lord for which thou hopest, at least speak to them with kindly speech: And let not thy hand be tied up to thy neck; nor yet open it with all openness, lest thou sit thee down in rebuke, in beggary.
>
> Verily, thy Lord will provide with open hand for whom he pleaseth, and will be sparing. His servants doth he scan, inspect. Kill not your children for fear of want: for them and for you will we provide. Verily, killing them is a great wickedness.
>
> Have naught to do with adultery; for it is a foul thing and an evil way: Neither slay any one whom God hath

forbidden you to slay; unless for a just cause: and whosoever shall be slain wrongfully, to his heir have we given powers; but let him not outstep bounds in putting the manslayer to death, for he too, in his turn, will be assisted and avenged.

And touch not the substance of the orphan, unless in an upright way, till he attain his age of strength: And perform your covenant; verily the covenant shall be enquired of: And give full measure when you measure, and weigh with just balance.

This will be better, and fairest for settlement: And follow not that of which thou hast no knowledge; because the hearing and the sight and the heart—each of these shall be enquired of: And walk not proudly on the earth, for thou canst not cleave the earth, neither shalt thou reach to the mountains in height: All this is evil; odious to thy Lord. This is part of the wisdom which thy Lord hath revealed to thee. Set not up any other god with God, lest thou be cast into Hell, rebuked, cast away.

Sura 17:23–40 (Koran)

The Koran gives no basis for believing what Muhammad wrote other than that it was given to him by a spirit in a dream. If the spirit had been from God the Almighty, then there would be no words passed down that would conflict with what he had already said in the old scriptures. Since all the teachings from Muhammad, conflict with the teachings of the Bible, then one can only assume that the spirit speaking to Muhammad was Satan, and therefore; a legitimate basis for not believing what is written in the Koran.

Muhammad told his biographer Ibn Ishaq that the Koran existed in heaven before it was given to him. The strange statement that it teaches by iteration as well as the lack of any mention of the Holy Spirit leads me to agree that the entire book existed in the spiritual realm prior to it's transmission to Muhammad. Why would any author writing for instruction admit to teaching by iteration? I surmise that the higher power required this revelation to be included in the book. I am reminded that the unforgivable sin is blasphemy against the Holy Spirit, so the author of the Koran refused to go there. That teaching is directly from Jesus in Luke 12:10:

> And everyone who speaks a word against the Son of Man, it will be forgiven him; but he who blasphemes against the Holy Spirit, it will not be forgiven him.
>
> Luke 12:10 (NASB)

During the prayer times there are certain movements and memorized sayings which are prescribed in the Koran. The Salat is the prayer ritual, and the following is copied from instructions published for the believer to learn that rite.

> And observe prayer at early morning, at the close of the day, and at the approach of night; for the good deeds drive away the evil deeds.
>
> Sura 11:116 (Koran)

> (Said after prostration) *And Say* "Praise be to God who hath not begotten a son, who hath no partner in the Kingdom, nor any protector on account of weakness." And magnify him by proclaiming His greatness.
>
> Sura 17:111 (Koran)

The words *"And Say,"* at the beginning of a verse indicate that God is indicating that we utter these specific words during our Salat. These words "Praise be to God who hath not begotten a son," purify us from the claim of the Christians who gave God a son.

Denouncing Christianity continues in the pilgrimage that Muslims are urged to make to Mecca. In her book *Standing Alone*, Asra Q. Nomani gives a prayer that the participants in the

PORK, BEEF, CHICKEN AND RIBS

pilgrimage are supposed to chant as they walk to the Ka'bah, that is called the talbiya.

> Labayk! (Here I am at your service!)
> Allahumma labayk. (At your service, oh Lord.)
> Labayk. (Here I am at your service.)
> La shareeka laka. (No partner do you have.)
> Labayk. (Here I come.)
> Innal hamda wan ni'mata. (Praise indeed and blessings are yours.)
> Laka wal mulk. (And the dominion.)
> La shareeka laka. (No partner do you have.)

All the pilgrims know that the term "no partner do you have," is denouncing the trinity, and therefore denouncing Jesus as the Christ, and Christianity. Sura 9:34–35 must be included in any instruction about the Koran. This teaching requires that a believer be willing to expend their total wealth to promote the cause of their God.

> O believers! Of a truth, many of the teachers and monks do devour man's substance in vanity and turn them from the way of God. But to those who treasure up gold and silver and expend it not in the way of God, announce tidings of a grievous torment. On That Day (resurrection) their treasures shall be heated in Hell-fire, and their foreheads, and their sides, and their backs, shall be branded with them…. "This is what ye have treasured up for yourselves; taste, therefore, your treasures!"
>
> Sura 9:35–36 (Koran)

Fain would the wicked redeem himself from punishment on That Day (resurrection) at the price of his children, of his spouse and his brother, and of his kindred who showed affection for him, and of all who are on the earth that then it might deliver him. But no. For the Fire, dragging by the scalp, shall claim him who turned his back and went away, and amassed and hoarded.

Sura 70:11–18 (Koran)

Not so the prayerful, who are ever constant at their prayers; and of whose substance there is a due and stated portion for him who asketh, and for him who is ashamed to beg; and who own the Judgment Day a truth, and who thrill with dread at the chastisement of their Lord—For there is none safe from the chastisement of their Lord.

Sura 70: 22–28 (Koran)

THE CHRISTIAN BIBLE

INTRODUCTION

When you study the Bible there are parts that are very plain spoken and easy to understand, and parts that are difficult to understand. In order to decipher what prophesy is included within a book, we must recognize the significant portion of the writings just as in listening to a professor in a classroom situation; there is always some difference in tone for subjects dear to his heart.

I want to use the book of Amos as an example of this change in tone, or emphasis. Amos was one of the earliest prophets and his writings make it possible to date them to 760–750 BC and the NASB dates the book of Amos during that time. Most of Amos writings relate to the people of that time with few unusual passages. Amos tells of a famine for the word of God, and this prophesy is obviously for future times (Amos 8: 11–12). The only other noticeable passage in Amos that is for future times is the Lord telling of the new Israel in Amos 9:14–15.

> Behold, days are coming, declares the Lord God, "When I will send a famine on the land, Not a famine for bread or a thirst for water, but rather for hearing the words of the Lord. "People will stagger from sea to sea and from the

north even to the east; they will go to and fro to seek the word of the Lord, but they will not find it.

Amos 8:11–12 (NASB)

Also I will restore the captivity of my people Israel, and they will rebuild the ruined cities and live in them; they will also plant vineyards and drink their wine, and make gardens and eat their fruit. "I will also plant them on their land, and they will not again be rooted out from their land which I have given them," says the Lord your God.

Amos 9:14–15 (NASB)

Throughout the Bible there are prophesies of what will occur in this world, and taken in their entirety they give a complete story of the development of our religion from the beginning to the end. There will be many who will disagree with my interpretations, and that is as it should be. We should all want to know what God has prescribed for us, his children, and we should all be willing to seek that knowledge through study of his Word. God made it very clear through Amos that, through his prophets, he would tell what was to happen before it came about. We find these prophesies through study of the Bible and can also read about the fulfillment of these prophesies from scripture written in later years. We can also recognize the fulfillment of Bible prophesies through the study of secular history. Isaiah also told about this characteristic of God.

I am the Lord, that is my name; I will not give my glory to another, nor my praise to graven images. Behold, the former things have come to pass, now I declare new things; before they spring forth I proclaim them to you.

Isaiah 42:8–9 (NASB)

Throughout the Bible we find the characteristics of God told by his prophets and also others that knew of his ways. Balaam, son of Beor, gave this discourse when asked by Balak, the king of Moab, what the Lord had spoken.

> God is not a man, that he should lie, nor a son of man, that he should repent; has he said, and will he not do it? Or has he spoken, and will he not make it good?
>
> Numbers 23:19 (NASB)

By this passage we know that God will do what he promises. Daniel, John the Baptist, the Apostle John, and the Apostle Paul have all contributed to the collage of end-time prophesy that gives us expectation of an eminent return of the Lord. Daniel sees the future coming of Jesus and the final conflict, in his vision reported in chapter 7.

> I kept looking in the night visions, and behold, with the clouds of heaven one like a Son of Man was coming, and he came up to the Ancient of Days and was presented before him. And to him was given dominion, glory, and a kingdom, that all the peoples, nations, and men of every language might serve him. His dominion is an everlasting dominion which will not pass away; and his kingdom is one which will not be destroyed.
>
> Daniel 13–14 (NASB)

INTERPRETATION OF THE BIBLE

There is a controversy about the interpretation of Bible scripture. One school of thought believes in a literal translation or a take-it-as-it-is written approach, to which I subscribe. The only other theory of interpretation that I am aware of is called the "Higher Criticism Theory." There must be a third theory that I do not know, but I do get some indication it of by discussing the Bible with my Presbyterian pastor.

Recently, he called the book of Jonah a fable, and I reminded him of what Jesus had said that just as Jonah was three days in the belly of a great fish, so must he be three days in the heart of the earth. I could have added what Jesus said about the book of Jonah another time (Matt. 12:41, Luke 11:32) saying, "The men of Nineveh will stand up with this generation at the judgment, and will condemn it because they repented at the preaching of Jonah; and behold, something greater than Jonah is here."

In my opinion we should accept the story of Jonah as actually occurring because that is what Jesus intimated. Jesus promised his disciples that the Holy Spirit would bring to their remembrance, all that he had said to them (John 14:26 NASB).

He had also explained all the scriptures in the Old Testament that related to him to two of his disciples on the road to Emmaus, and then told them that "all things which are written about me in the Law of Moses and the Prophets and the Psalms must be fulfilled" (Luke 24:27, 44, NASB). Any serious Bible scholar can recognize these scriptures and determine whether they have been fulfilled or not.

The Apostle Paul was taught by Christ Jesus and was shown visions of what was to happen in future times. The relationship between Jesus, the risen Lord, and Apostle Paul is important, and a special section will be used to cover this story. We should know that what these disciples wrote for us is true. Apostle Paul also said that all scriptures are inspired by God (2 Timothy 3:16 NASB). All of these passages support a literal translation.

The higher criticism theory of Biblical Interpretation became the norm for theological institutions sometime in the early nineteenth century. The principles used are those used for literary interpretation of a secular writing such as a history or autobiography. The higher criticism theory holds that the Bible is inaccurate on many points and is not historically reliable; moreover, it assumes that the prophets could not have any supernatural ability to foretell the future, even though the prophets claimed to be reporting what God spoke to them, and even though Christ himself verified the accuracy of their writings.

The theory, therefore, when applied to the Bible denies that the Scriptures are inspired by God. To call this theory *higher* is simply doublespeak to make an anti-Christian religious theory to sound palatable. You cannot subscribe to this "*higher* criticism theory and believe that Christ is God. The Antichrist will be an ardent supporter of this theory, for this is an assault by ungodly forces against Christianity. Their reason is simple. There can be no respect for a non-Christian religion as long as the Bible, as we know it, is deemed to be authoritative.

Doublespeak is the term given to language that is deliberately constructed to disguise or distort its actual meaning. Good examples of this doublespeak is the use of *downsizing*, for the firing of many people; *tough questioning*, for torture, and protective custody, for imprisonment without due process.

We encounter doublespeak in advertising, in political and religious rhetoric, and propaganda. Doublespeak is normally used when the true meaning of a term is concealed by the use of words with a meaning understood only by people who know the code. Words or phrases are applied to atrocious acts to make them sound more acceptable, such as *ethnic cleansing*, for genocide; or *combat fatigue*, for shell shock. These are euphemisms that a person reading a document must learn, in order to garner the true meaning presented in the document.

Euphemism: The substitution of an agreeable or inoffensive expression for one that may offend or suggest something unpleasant. I deem "Higher Criticism Theory" to be doublespeak.

In the 1920s, conservative Christians were assaulted with the new ideas from the Modernist who subscribed to the "Higher Criticism" theory of literary interpretation. The Modernists gained control of Princeton Theological Seminary in 1929, resulting in the resignation of three of their most noted theologians: Oswald Thompson Allis, J. Gresham Machen, and Robert Dick Wilson; and the subsequent formation of the Westminster Theological Seminary by these distinguished theologians. Westminster still holds to the literary interpretation of the scriptures, and is a bastion of conservative Christian theology. Cornelius Van Til joined the exodus from Princeton and became an outspoken critic of the Higher Criticism Theory and said that it must omit much of the Bible.

ACCURACY OF THE BIBLE

Why do I think that the Bible, which I study, is God's word handed down through the ages? The book itself claims to be from God, and makes reference to what God has said throughout the book. God also established a system to insure the accuracy of the scriptures so that everyone would be taught from the same source. Of the twelve tribes of Israel God separated one tribe, the tribe of Levi, to be the priest and workers in the institution of religion; with provisions to compensate them for this service. The Levites became the priest and the scribes and one of their responsibilities was to insure accuracy of the scriptures.

They had strict guidelines for duplicating the scriptures and therefore, to insure the accuracy of new copies. A single error was cause to destroy the entire scroll. The original manuscripts were written on prepared animal skin called parchment, which would deteriorate with age and use. It was, therefore, mandatory, that new scrolls be made periodically and this became the job for the Scribes. They developed detailed rules for reproducing the scrolls, from the selection of the parchment, to completion of the complete scroll; even to counting the number of characters on a page. Special rooms were designed to facilitate the copying process, and archeological excavations have found these facilities with ink still in the inkwells. Accurate reproduction of the scriptures was given a high priority in the every day labor of the Jewish temple, and the scribes were highly respected for their work.

When the Romans destroyed the temple in Jerusalem in AD 70, the place for the meeting of the Sanhedrin was moved to Jamnia, a town near the Palestinian coast south of Jaffa, known today as Yabneh. It is likely that the temple scrolls were also moved there to the famous Jewish rabbinical school of the Pharisees known as the School of Johanan ben Zakkai. It is known that the Great Sanhedrin would meet there. Faced with the dangers of war with the Romans and a growing apostasy in favor of the Christian belief, the Sanhedrin went about to establish an accurate traditional copy of all the scriptures, our Old Testament, and then selected a group of dedicated priest and scribes to take charge of the scriptures, and to take them to a safe location, and to keep them accurate. This they did and continued to do until the tenth century. The last of these Masoretic (Traditional) manuscripts was dated AD 916 and became the accepted source for the present day Old Testament as we know it. The Jews were well aware that a famine for the word of God was prophesied by Amos (Amos 8:11–12 NASB), and they were determined that it not happen on their watch.

There arose criticism from other forms of religions about the correctness of the Christian belief. This criticism came from the adherents of the Gnostic and Monophysitic variation because it served their purpose to cast doubt in order to sway adherents to their way of thinking. The adherents to these uninspired religions wrote many manuscripts to promote their agenda and these were circulating during the early years of the second century. Many of these writings became intertwined with the Christian belief or portions of the story of Jesus, and resulted in many scriptures available throughout the land that was incorrect, incomplete, or completely heretical.

A brilliant and wealthy Greek adherent to Christianity by the name of Marcion, came to Rome in AD 120–130 and worked to determine, which of the many available Christian texts were valid and which were not. He authenticated the writings of Paul that we know today. He was instrumental to the selection of an approved canon of the New Testament scripture that was necessary to protect the faith from heresy. The content of the New Testament as we know it today was finalized at the Council of Carthage in 419. The authorities responsible for maintaining sameness in the Bible scriptures have been very successful. In 1948 the discovery of the Dead Sea Scrolls proved that the Essene sect of Judaism had scriptural text of the Old Testament that were essentially the same that we have today. These scrolls were carbon dated to the first century, and it is believed that the Essenes placed the scrolls into the protective jars and into the caves to protect them from the invading Roman armies.

When Marcion began his work to canonize the New Testament, his first desire was to do away with or eliminate the Old Testament entirely. That would have been a serious mistake for the new faith, because both books are necessary to fully comprehend God's plan of salvation, and his great love for mankind–all mankind. The Old Testament authenticates God's plan and provides us with insight on his thinking. The importance of the Old Testament Scripture was evident to the followers of Jesus. His Disciple Peter tells us that no prophesy was ever made by an act of human will, but men moved by the Holy Spirit spoke from God (2 Pet. 1:20–21 NASB). Apostle Paul goes even farther and says that all Scriptures are inspired by God (2 Tim. 3:16 NASB). It is also important to note that Peter was telling of being with Jesus during the transfiguration, and of hearing the voice of God say; "this is my beloved Son with whom I am well pleased."

And Peter then writes for our benefit: "So we have the prophetic word made more sure, to which you do well to pay

PORK, BEEF, CHICKEN AND RIBS

attention" (2 Pet. 1:19 NASB), and then he tells us that he is writing to us for a reminder, "that you should remember the words spoken beforehand by the holy prophets, and the commandments of the Lord and Savior spoken by your apostles." These are the apostles of Christ, urging you to study God's word. This is our Lord and Savior saying to us (Matt. 11:29 NASB): "Take my yoke upon you and learn from me, and I will give you rest for your souls."

The writer of the letter to the Hebrews references Old Testament scripture many times. I find twenty-nine separate quotations from the Old Testament included in the book of Hebrews, most (eleven) from the Psalms, four from Isaiah, three each from Exodus and Deuteronomy, two each from Genesis and Jeremiah, and single references from 2 Samuel, Proverbs, Habakkuk, and Haggai. The Old Testament then is a very important part of our knowledge about the Almighty God and his likes and dislikes. It is in the Old Testament that we find God's plan to make salvation available to all people, all over the world.

The most definite proof that the Old Testament portion of our Bible is accurate came with the discovery of the Dead Sea Scrolls in 1947. These ancient manuscripts found stored in caves in the Judeaian wilderness area known as Qumran, have provided original manuscripts in Hebrew of most of the Old Testament and have been carbon dated to the AD first century. Every book of the OT except Ester is represented among these treasures. The find set off a flurry of searches which have resulted in significant findings in eleven caves, consisting of at least four hundred manuscripts. There were twelve Isaiah scrolls found in cave four alone, along with thirteen of Deuteronomy, ten of Psalms, and a well-preserved manuscript of the Book of Samuel. The handwritten scrolls were the most valuable property of the Jewish congregations, and there was apparently a mass effort to protect the scrolls from the invading Roman armies of AD 70, and/or during the second Jewish revolt AD 132–135. The Romans apparently destroyed any religious manuscripts which they found. The significance of this find was summed up by Charles F. Pfeiffer on page 111 of his book "The Dead Sea Scrolls and the Bible," by this statement: "While the Dead Sea Scrolls can neither prove nor disprove inspiration, they clearly indicate that a community of Jews more that nineteen centuries ago possessed a library of sacred writings which in all essential details is the same as the Bible which we have regarded as authoritative." With this irrefutable proof, I am assured that the New American Standard Bible which I use is as near the original scripture as any available publication. The Reverend, Dr. Charles F Stanley, of "In Touch" Ministries said of the NASB: "Over the course of more than fifty years of study, I have used nearly every available version and translation of the Bible. There is not a more accurate translation than the New American Standard Bible." If you have been taught from any source other than the Holy Bible, previously described as translated from the Masoretic Text, then you may want to compare what you have been taught with this approved scripture.

God's displeasure with the nation of Israel is told throughout the prophets from Amos through Malachi, and all prophesied about the destruction of Jerusalem and the scattering of the people throughout the world, commanded by God in Amos 9:9. This prophesy was fulfilled when the nation of Israel rebelled against the Roman empire in AD 70, and after being completely defeated, the Jews were made to leave Jerusalem. The land upon which God had placed the children of Israel following the Exodus was given over to other nations, and there was no country named for them until the nation was reconstituted by the United Nations following World War II. Also prophesied throughout the old testament prophets is the gathering back of the people of Israel into their own land, and usually this prophesy relates to the new Israel of God, rather than the descendants of Abraham. The teachings of the Apostle Paul in Romans indicate that ancestral Israel was scattered because of their unbelief. The new Israel, we, Christians, who have demonstrated a favorable reaction to God's plan of salvation, have been gathered together into our own land—this land of freedom and justice for all, the United States of America.

The Bible is a complete mystery to many people, and that is not a good situation. It is a good thing for a person to want to learn what God prefers for them to do, and he promises many benefits to those who will learn of him. God gives us a mind of our own and the freedom to seek knowledge and truth about anything in this world. He will guide us through this life if we want that, but he will never demand that we follow his teachings. I have found that God also has a requirement for us who have gained understanding to pass along what we have learned. God made this very clear to Jeremiah by telling him that; "let him who has my Word, speak my word in truth,"(Jer. 23:28 NASB).

The modern Bible is easily understood. Many times I have been amazed to find a passage that I did not understand, to be rephrased, and repeated a second time in such a way that my understanding was enhanced. Occasionally, the Bible uses allegory, and the metaphor must be recognized; and one good example is the word "sword," to mean God's righteous indignation. All the people who are said to "die by the sword," are not necessarily thrust through, but simply die without the benefit of God's protection, or influence in their lives. The word "wisdom," used in the book of Proverbs, denotes a belief in God, or a mind that is accepting of God's teachings. A large portion of the Bible is devoted to history, and it is a history of only the Hebrew people or Israel. While this historical record is necessary to ferret out the finer details of prophesy or theology, it is not required for the beginner seeking the right belief to follow. I will attempt to give the reader a summary of the important teachings of the Bible without the more detailed history and prophesy, which are not prerequisites to student beginners.

It is very helpful to know what the Bible teaches in order to recognize theology that is not Christian or that opposes Christianity. Many people who think that they know what the Bible teaches are going on the assumption that the God of the Bible is a benevolent God that will pardon all good people. At the opposite extreme, there are those, who think that they are never to attain the level of righteousness that is necessary to be pleasing to God. They think that they know what the Bible teaches without ever having studied it. There seems to be a reluctance on the part of many people to learn the truth because they worry that they will have to alter their lifestyle. The rewards of learning about God's teachings are manifold. First, there is nothing for you to be worried about when you study God's word. Only good things such as peace of mind, security, and happiness will result when you learn what he desires of you. There is nothing to be feared from studying the Bible.

There are many religions in the world that have good people working to improve their communities and their religions. Even the believers of the pagan religions were respected citizens and influential in the communities to which they belonged. Most all religions teach similar ideas of what is good and what is evil, and many publish their theology in a book which adherents study as we study the Bible. The Baha'i Faith is a Persian alternative to the Muslim religion and may be similar to Christianity with a one god theology and a god similar to Christ, the Baha'u'llah, and a book of theology said to be from him teaches good things and include a monophysite god. Their theology accepts Jesus as a prophet, but denies his deity and the Christian Trinity, and this enhances their acceptance in Muslim nations.

In America, the Mormon faith has increased significantly since its founding in the early 1800s and presents itself as being Christian; however, some of the theology presented indicates otherwise. The Mormons believe that God was once human like us and that if we are good enough, we can become like God. This is expressed in a saying; "As I am now, God once was; As God is now I may become." This belief drives the adherents to strive for holiness and neophytes devote two years to mission work seeking new believers. Young men traveling in pairs on bicycles throughout the countryside (throughout the world) attempt to recruit new members.

The church claims to believe the Bible and accepts the Holy Spirit and Jesus just as Christians do; but they add The Book of Mormon and an angel named Maroni which must be accepted belief. They have built a network of temples throughout this country and those of the membership that are good enough can use these temples to pray for forgiveness of sins for their ancestors, which results in a more holy position for them. In order to determine who a person's ancestors are, the church has developed the most complete genealogical database available anywhere.

TEACHINGS FROM THE BIBLE

The Holy Bible covers the history of God and his interaction with humankind. According to the Bible, God created all things, which includes humankind. We are endowed with a mind that allows us to choose what we will do, and where we will walk, and what we will believe. This trait is referred to as "free will," and this characteristic causes us to respond to both good and evil influence. God's teaching is summed up very well by Isaiah.

> Learn to do good; seek justice, reprove the ruthless defend the orphan, plead for the widow. Come now, and let us reason together, says the Lord. Though your sins are as scarlet, they will be white as snow. Though they are red like crimson, they will be like wool. If you consent and obey, you will eat the best of the land; but if you refuse and

rebel, you will be devoured by the sword. Truly, the mouth of the Lord has spoken.

Isaiah 1:17–20 (NASB)

God desires our love and respect; however, without our being free to choose, that response would be meaningless. It is this "free will" that allows us to make our bad decisions such as those we'd rather not mention. We get to know God by studying the Bible. Through the study of the scriptures we can learn the personality of God from the ways he has reacted to people in the past, and by what he has written for us in the scriptures through his prophets. We know God to be omnipotent, which simply means all powerful; and he is omniscient, which just means that he is possessed with complete knowledge (He knows everything! Just what you would expect of God.); and he is omnipresent, or present at all places at all times.

He made us a promise that where two or three are gathered together in his name, that he will be there also. He claims to be the only God. He tells us that he is a jealous God and prohibits us from worshipping any other god, or any man-made image representing himself or any other god. The characteristics of God will always be the same because he does not change, and he cannot tell a lie. God first established that he is the only God through Moses; and many other times throughout the Bible.

> See now that I, I am he, and there is no god besides me; It is I who put to death and give life. I have wounded and it is I who heal, and there is no one who can deliver from my hand. Indeed, I lift up my hand to heaven and say, as I live forever, if I sharpen my flashing sword, and my hand takes hold on justice, I will render vengeance on my adversaries and I will repay those who hate me.
>
> Deuteronomy 32:39–41 (NASB)

Hannah sang a song while dedicating Samuel to the Lord.

> There is no one holy like the Lord, indeed, there is no one besides you, nor is there any rock like our God.
>
> 1 Samuel 2:2 (NASB)

> I am the Lord, and there is no other; besides me there is no God. I will gird you, though you have not known me; that men may know from the rising to the setting of the sun that there is no one besides me. I am the Lord, and there is no other.
>
> Isaiah 45:5–7 (NASB)

> Declare and set forth your case; indeed, let them consult together. Who has announced this from of old? Who has long since declared it? Is it not I, the Lord? And there is no other God besides me, a righteous God and a Savior; there is none except me. Turn to me and be saved, all the ends of the earth; for I am God and there is no other. I have sworn by myself, the word has gone forth from my mouth in righteousness and will not turn back, that to me every knee will bow, every tongue will swear allegiance.
>
> Isaiah 21–23 (NASB)

> Remember this, and be assured; recall it to mind, you transgressors. Remember the former things long past, for I am God, and there is no other; I am God, and there is no one like me, declaring the end from the beginning, and from ancient times things which have not been done, saying, 'my purpose will be established, and I will accomplish all my good pleasure.
>
> Isaiah 46:8–10

What you have just read are God's words sent down through his prophets, and are copied directly from the New American Standard Bible. The Bible is much more than just a theological document—it is a history of actual occurrences which are verified by secular writings and archeological findings. A stele of Rameses II, includes a phrase claiming that he "built Rameses with Asiatic Semetic (Hebrew) slaves," offers physical evidence of the Exodus story. A stele from his successor Pharaoh Merneptah mentions the departure of the Israelites from Egypt.

The Moabite Stone tells what a king wanted to pass along for his posterity and the inscription reads: "I, Mesha, King of Moab, made this monument to Chemosh (his god) to commemorate deliverance from Israel. My father reigned over Moab thirty years, and I reigned after my father. Omri, king of Israel, oppressed Moab many days and his son after him. But I warred against the king of Israel, and drove him out, and took his cities, Medeba, Ataroth, Nebo and Jahaz, which he built while he waged war against me. I destroyed his cities, and devoted the spoil to Chemosh, and the women and girls to Ashtar. I built Qorhah with prisoners from Israel. In Beth-Diblathaim, I placed sheep raisers."

People in powerful positions left their legacy on stone, monuments to themselves, and messages between these people were cast into clay tablets and many of them have survived. Thousands of ancient pieces have let us know how the people lived in Biblical times. The evidence is sufficient to prove that the Bible is a true historic document. Names of places have changed over the years and a good Bible Dictionary is a great help to understanding the Bible. Virtually, all of the Bible has verification from secular history and more is being learned as archeologists continue to dig into newly discovered ancient deposits. More can be learned about Biblical Archeology through reading on the subject in reference books or from the Internet.

PROPHESY IN THE BIBLE

It is helpful to know secular history and also history of religion in order to recognize the fulfillment of biblical prophecy. Most of biblical prophecy is concerned with secular issues, and intended for a specific time and place. There is very little biblical prophecy that remains unfulfilled. Some words used in the Old Testament can be misleading without some interpretation. One word that needs interpretation is "destroy." When God said "My people are destroyed for lack of knowledge," the destruction is damage to their souls. I also see a similar modification of the word destroy when the destruction of those countries rejecting God's ways is forecast; that destruction can be only in the moral or religious fiber of the nation. The sword of God is a figure of speech denoting his righteous indignation, not a sword with which to slay the Romans. The use of allegory confuses readers until they learn the definition of the words; but, through the use of allegory and parables, the stories become timeless. Some other interesting words that have different meanings from the way they are used today are found in these new covenant prophesies. God will not destroy horses as such; he will, however, do away with the military paraphernalia needed to wage war from those who would wage war with his people. Now read Micah 5:10 –15 and you will understand it more:

> It will be in that day, 'declares the Lord,' that I will cut off your horses from among you and destroy your chariots. I will also cut off the cities (fortified centers) of your land and tear down all your fortifications. I will cut off sorceries from your hand, and you will have fortune-tellers no more. I will cut off your carved images and your sacred pillars from among you, so that you will no longer bow down to the work of your hands. I will root out your Asherim (replicas of the goddess Ashtaroth, or the trees or poles

symbolizing her, and used in the worship of this female counterpart of Baal.) from among you and destroy your cities. And I will execute vengeance in anger and wrath on the nations which have not obeyed.

Micah 5:10 –15 (NASB)

If you continue reading through Micah you will find what the Lord requires of the new Israel at 6:8, and then the effects of the new covenant upon those who reject the covenant at 6:9 –16. This is such a good example of new covenant scripture that I will dwell on it.

With what shall I come to the Lord and bow myself before the God on high? Shall I come to him with burnt offerings, with yearling calves? Does the Lord take delight in thousands of rams, in ten thousand rivers of oil? Shall I present my firstborn for my rebellious acts, the fruit of my body for the sins of my soul? He has told you, O man, what is good; and what does the Lord require of you but to do justice, to love kindness, and to walk humbly with your God.

Micah 6:6 –8 (NASB)

This passage makes it clear that animal sacrifice will not be required for the new Israel. Now read about that part of the population who do not join in Gods covenant.

The voice of the Lord will call to the city—and it is sound wisdom to fear your name: Hear O tribe. Who has appointed its time? Is there yet a wicked man in the wicked house, along with treasures of wickedness and a short measure that is cursed? For the rich men of the city are full of violence, her residents speak lies, and their tongue is deceitful in their mouth. So also I will make you sick, striking you down, desolating you because of your sins. You will eat, but you will not be satisfied, and your vileness will be in your midst. You will try to remove for safekeeping, but you will not preserve anything, and what you do preserve I will give to the sword. You will sow but you will not reap. You will tread the olive but you will not anoint yourself with oil; and the grapes, but you will not drink the wine. The statues of Omri and all the works of the house of Ahab (altar for worship of Baal.) are observed; and in their devices you walk. Therefore, I will give you up for destruction and your inhabitants for derision, and you will bear the reproach of my people.

Micah 6:9–16 (NASB)

There is no good thing promised by God for those who do not take hold of his offer of salvation.

The conflict that exists in the world today is the same conflict between good and evil that has existed since the time of Adam and Eve. All the components of this conflict are told about in the Bible but to find those components requires a lot of study, both in the Bible, and history of religions, as well as secular history. I will attempt to clarify the component parts that make up the story of this conflict for the benefit of my Christian brothers, and hopefully inform those who are not Christian of the workings of the Almighty God, so that they might become Christians.

It has always been God's desire that all men would come to know him, and live a life pleasing to him; but Satan interferes with God's plans wherever he can, and seems to have had a fair amount of success. We know from the prophet Zechariah that only one in three will gain salvation and two thirds will be cut off and perish. Jesus himself described the greater portion going to destruction in his parable of the wide and narrow gates.

"Enter through the narrow gate; for the gate is wide and the way is broad that leads to destruction, and there are many who enter through it. For the gate is small and the way is narrow that leads to life and there are few who find it" (Matt. 7:13–14 NASB). The US Center for World Mission in a year 2000 report stated that 33 percent of the world population was Christians and the majority was concentrated in the United States. Consider this also, this equation from Zechariah likely will not only include those who are alive, but those who are in the graves as well.

> Awake, O sword, against my Shepherd, and against the man, my Associate," declares the Lord of host. "Strike the Shepherd that the sheep may be scattered; and I will turn My hand upon the little ones." "It will come about in all the land," declares the Lord, "that two parts in it will be cut off and perish; but the third will be left in it. And I will bring the third part through the fire, refine them as silver is refined, and test them as gold is tested. They will call on my name, and I will answer them; I will say, 'they are my people,' and they will say, 'The Lord is my God.
>
> Zechariah 13:7–9 (NASB)

These are words that were inspired by the Almighty God and written at his direction by the prophet Zechariah about five hundred years before God's Shepherd, who is Jesus Christ, was born. Bible scholars say that Zechariah wrote from 538 BC to 480 BC. Who are those who will be cut off and perish? We know that they will include the forces of evil, who oppose God's desires and hinder the work of his chosen people. Many of those who perish will be identified by the mark of the beast, the mark of Satan the Devil. Most of those who will perish are those that just did not believe God, or did not accept that God is real. The one part of three that will be refined and tested is the group made up of those who believe in God and accepts his plan for their salvation.

PORK, BEEF, CHICKEN AND RIBS

THE NEW COVENANT

When God spoke directly to the people assembled at Horeb, the words were so fearful to them that they asked Moses to speak to them what God said because they did not want to hear directly from the mouth of God anymore for fear of death. At that time, God told Moses of a new plan which he would use to interact with his people.

> The Lord said to me, "They have spoken well. I will raise up a prophet from among their countrymen like you, and I will put my words in his mouth, and he shall speak to them all that I command him. It shall come about that whoever will not listen to my words which he shall speak in my name, I myself will require it of him.
>
> Deuteronomy 18:17–19 (NASB)

This word given to Moses was the first indication of a new covenant between God and mankind; or in reality the entire universe because this new covenant was binding both on the spiritual and the physical worlds. That covenant is God's plan for the salvation of the world and is the central theme of the Christian story. The Apostle Peter interpreted Deuteronomy 18:19 this way: "and it will be that every soul that does not heed that prophet shall be utterly destroyed from among the people" (Acts 3:23 NASB).

The provisions of this new covenant need to be studied in detail, but first let's think about what God is saying when he said in Zechariah that he will refine us as silver is refined, and test us like gold is tested. The process of refining gold and silver involved heating the ore by fire until the metal liquefies and will pour away from the dross. The purity of Gold and silver was tested by submerging it in water to determine its volume by measuring the amount of water displaced, and then floating it in a vessel to determine its weight by the amount of water displaced by the vessel; then the specific gravity of the gold could be computed (the purity of it).

God is using a metaphor to describe the testing that you or I might be subjected to in our everyday lives. Assume that you are faced with the possibility of receiving a large sum of money, but you must tell a lie to receive it. You may be in God's refining process, and if you refuse to lie, you gain value in God's eyes. If you lie to receive the wealth, then you have been burned, you have been set aflame without recognizing the damage which it will cause you. The last verse in Isaiah 42 is God's final determination of the integrity of the nation Israel, and he uses this metaphor of being refined.

The cessation of the prophets is forecast several times in the Old Testament and the time established for the end of the prophets was to coincide with the time of the initiation of the new covenant. Jesus confirms that John the Baptist was the last of the prophets (Matt. 11:13 NASB) by saying that, "all the prophets and the law, prophesied until John". Considering these definite biblical teachings, it is logical to say that any person claiming to be a prophet after John is a false prophet. God has warned us about false prophets, or people who claim that they have a revelation from him when they do not have. In about 587 BC, Jeremiah was prophesying for God in Jerusalem, and there were other influential religious leaders opposing him and declaring their own belief which was contrary to what God had told Jeremiah to say. Here is what God said at that time about false prophets.

> I have heard what the prophets have said who prophesy falsely in my name, saying, 'I had a dream, I had a dream!' How long? Is there anything in the hearts of the prophets who prophesy falsehood, even these prophets of the deception of their own heart, who intend to make my people forget my name by their dreams which they

relate to one another, just as their fathers forgot my name because of Baal?

The prophet who has a dream may relate his dream, but let him who has my word speak my word in truth. What does straw have in common with grain?" declares the lord. "Is not my word like fire?" declares the Lord, "and like a hammer which shatters a rock? Therefore behold, I am against the prophets," declares the Lord, "who steal my words from each other. Behold, I am against the prophets," declares the Lord, "who use their tongues and declare, 'the lord declares.' Behold, I am against those who have prophesied false dreams," declares the Lord, "and related them and led my people astray by their falsehoods and reckless boasting: yet I did not send them or command them, nor do they furnish this people the slightest benefit, declares the Lord.

Jeremiah 23:25–32 (NASB)

This word is from God through Jeremiah, twenty seven hundred years ago, is just as applicable today. Any religion that teaches a belief that does not conform to the teachings of the Holy Bible constitutes a false teaching. Recall the word from God about false prophets when he said,"but let him who has my word speak my word in truth."

If Jeremiah had failed to speak out, then he would have been disobeying God; for God had told him, "but let him who has my word speak my word in truth." Notice also that the statement is for all people who have God's word. In order for someone to speak out, they must be qualified to do so. How can we speak out unless we know what is right to say? We must prepare ourselves by learning what God desires through study of the Bible. God prescribes that we study to make ourselves approved by him.

This warning God gave after the new covenant was ratified is a warning against the religion which will come from Satan's inspiration which is Islam. Notice the repetitive, "I have a dream," which is indicative of the repetitive nature of the Koran. The evil warned about is the same evil that sponsored the past worship of Baal, a false religion that preyed on the human sex drive, and provided temple prostitutes to attract men to join the cult. Jezebell, the wife of King Ahab, was considered a prophetess to that cult. There is no warning against any other evil because it is the same Satan known since the beginning of man in the Garden of Eden.

Another warning of deceptive repetitive scripture comes from Jeremiah 7:4. The "apostasy" that Paul warns about in 2 Thessalonians, is the final opposition prophesied in the Bible, and be well aware that this opposition will last until the end of this age, and also be aware that signs of the end abound in today's conflict. This thought reminds me of a writing on a tombstone that I found in a very old cemetery: "Remember friend as you pass by as you are now so once was I. As I am now so you will be. Prepare yourself to follow me." This thought leads to Paul's statement that there is no name under the sun by which you can be saved except the name of Jesus Christ, our Lord. The new covenant that God has made with the universe is fixed, and it is narrow, and it is the wisdom of the true God.

A covenant is a pledge or a contract between two or more parties, and the parties are bound to perform the obligation expressed in the covenant. The covenant which we are to study is a contract made by God, and establishes what he will do in the lives of those affected by the covenant. When God bound himself by this covenant to you and I, we had absolutely no input about what the covenant requires or what it provides.

This covenant which we study is called new because there was a covenant made between God and Abraham that now must be referred to as the old covenant. The old covenant involved only God as one party, and Abraham and his descendants as the other party. The old covenant was not optional on the part of

Abraham's descendants—the Jews. The new covenant is between God and any person in the entire world that chooses to believe him, and is optional; it can be ignored, or rejected, or accepted. This new covenant first mentioned to Moses in Deuteronomy was referenced by Jesus in John 5:46 when he told the Sanhedrin that Moses wrote of him. It is told about in more detail by Jeremiah.

> Behold, days are coming, declares the Lord, "when I will make a new covenant with the house of Israel and with the house of Judah, not like the covenant which I made with their fathers in the day I took them by the hand to bring them out of the land of Egypt, my Covenant which they broke, although I was a husband to them," declares the Lord. "But this is the covenant which I will make with the house of Israel after those days," declares the Lord, "I will put my law within them and on their heart I will write it; and I will be their God, and they shall be my people. "They will not teach again each man his neighbor and each man his brother, saying, 'Know the Lord,' for they will all know me, from the least of them to the greatest of them," declares the Lord, "for I will forgive their iniquity, and their sin I will remember no more.
>
> Jeremiah 31:31–34 (NASB)

Notice that this passage of scripture only mentions what God will do for the house of Israel, and does not tell of the obligations which the house of Israel must assume to become a party to this covenant. Notice also that the covenant is only described and not yet begun. "Behold, days are coming," indicates a future time. The most valuable provision of this covenant is the last part: "for I will forgive their iniquity, and their sin I will remember no more." This promise from God is for salvation, and since salvation is a personal condition, this places this covenant between God on the one hand and an individual such as you or I on the other. Because this covenant is not fully explained in a single location in the Bible, makes our study about it necessary. Think of how God might instill his laws within us or write them on our hearts. I think perhaps that he was looking forward to the day of the Pentecost and the gift of the Holy Spirit. The next part of this new covenant is mentioned later by Jeremiah.

> Behold, days are coming, declares the Lord, "when I will fulfill the good word which I have spoken concerning the house of Israel and the house of Judah. In those days and at that time I will cause a righteous Branch of David to spring forth; and he shall execute justice and righteousness on earth.
>
> Jeremiah 33:14–15 (NASB)

By this passage we know that this new covenant will be placed into effect along with the appearance of the Messiah. The greatest significance is the latter part: "and he shall execute justice and righteousness on earth," because this tells that the salvation afforded through this covenant will be executed in the whole world. Now review what these passages mean to you and I. God will provide salvation to any person in the whole world (on earth), who will qualify and in doing so will forgive their past sins and never remember sins which they subsequently commit. We do not know at the time of this writing, the contractual requirements to become a party to his covenant, but we do know that a righteous branch of David, the Messiah, will be the executor. We know now that this new covenant was begun seven hundred years after the prophecy in Jeremiah and Jesus of Nazareth was the Branch of David and God's own right arm.

Remember now that the purpose of the New Covenant is to offer salvation to all mankind; to anyone and anywhere in the world, and the beginning of this new covenant coincides with the appearance of the righteous Branch of the family of David, who is Jesus Christ. Therefore, this new covenant has been in effect

PORK, BEEF, CHICKEN AND RIBS

for about the last two thousand years. Another provision of the new covenant is an end to the prophets, sorcerers, diviners, and witchcraft. All of the interaction between man and God, and man and Satan, that had gone on since the beginning of civilization, would be changed. No longer could evil spirits possess the human mind, nor would special talents be permitted so that a person in the physical world could contact the spiritual world. Objections from the evil part of the spiritual world were probably the only impediments to God initiating his plan. Jesus and his apostles cast out evil spirits from people possessed by them, and multitudes of these occurrences are recorded in New Testament narratives. We are accustomed to the new order and never think of the supernatural powers which were once well known. Gone from our minds also are the names of the pagan gods worshipped throughout civilization two thousand years ago. Zechariah 13:2 foretells the elimination of idols, prophets, and unclean spirits.

> It will come to about in that day, declares the Lord of hosts, that I will cut off the names of the idols from the land, and they will no longer be remembered: and I will also remove the prophets and the unclean spirit from the land.
>
> Zechariah 13:2 (NASB)

A similar prophesy is made in Micah and obviously, a wider separation between the spiritual realm and the physical world was initiated with the new covenant.

> I will also cut off sorceries from your hand, and you will have fortune-tellers no more. I will cut off your carved images and your sacred pillars from among you, so that you will no longer bow down to the work of your hands.
>
> Micah 5:12–13 (NASB)

One well publicized provision that is part of the new covenant include the elimination of evil spirits which could invade the minds of human beings, and a multitude of exorcisms are reported in the New Testament. It is interesting to note that in every instance where the spirit spoke that was being exorcized, that spirit was fully aware of who Jesus was. This indicates that the new covenant provisions were well known within the spiritual realm. Eliminated also were soothsayers, diviners, and prophets. These changes indicate a much wider separation between the spiritual realm and the physical world, than existed prior to the implementation of these new rules that was to be brought about by the new covenant. There is a spiritual realm to this universe that is told about in the Bible and must be recognized as being there by the people who believe in God, an all-powerful God, who formed the universe and controls its destiny.

We live within the physical realm and know that it is real, but the spiritual realm must be accessed by faith and seen only dimly and based only on that faith. Faith does not just flow into your mind automatically but must be searched for by learning what is right. The spiritual realm was more apparent to people before the time of Christ, and many examples are revealed throughout the Bible of people having special powers to contact the spiritual world. Described most often are the prophets of God. We are told of the commissioning of Isaiah, in detail, in chapter 6. We are also told of mediums or diviners in 1 Sam. 28:7–19, when Saul had a medium conjure up the spirit of Samuel. Because of what Samuel said we know that the medium had supernatural power. The first utterance of Samuel was, "Why have you disturbed me by bringing me up?" We know that Samuel was summoned against his will because he was bothered by the call-up. Balaam son of Beor, was a well-known diviner during the time of Moses, and his exploits are told about in Numbers chapters 22 and 23.

SUMMARY OF THE OLD TESTAMENT

Throughout the history of the nation of Israel there have been prophets who received word from God of what would happen in the future. The prophets were authenticated by their forecast occurring. Here is a list of prophets that are named in the Old Testament: Moses, Samuel, Elijah, Elisha, Jonah, Amos, Hosea, Joel, Isaiah, Micah, Obadiah, Nahum, Jeremiah, Habakkuk, Zephaniah, Daniel, Ezekiel, Zechariah, and probably Malachi.

Most of the prophets from Moses onward told of portions of the new covenant. The new covenant applies to all people of the world and makes many provisions that we can only recognize by the resulting changes that have occurred. This covenant is called new because there was a covenant made between God and Abraham that now must be referred to as the old covenant. When we study the history of religion, a picture emerges of the drastic changes that came about when the age of the new covenant began. In order to understand the new covenant, it is necessary to be familiar with the old one.

Here is a short explanation. The old covenant was made with Abraham and involved only Abraham and his descendants. These people were to be a witness of God, and they accomplished this by faithfully recording the interaction between God and themselves, and the culmination of their mission was this history of God in a written form we call the "Old Testament." Today anyone who has the desire to know God can learn of him by reading the record produced by Abraham and his descendants.

The most important thing to remember about the old covenant is that it was made by God, and was his contract made with the descendants of Abraham and applied to all Israel. The old covenant was mandatory. The new covenant is not, and it is available to all people of the world who choose to take hold of it. To take hold of the new covenant is simply to believe God, trust in him, and follow his instructions which are found in the Bible; and through this covenant, salvation is made available to all mankind. I want to provide here, the prophetic scripture that tells the provisions of the new covenant, and give you my layman's explanation of God's plan.

God's plan is to provide salvation to all people. In order to understand this contract God has made with us, you need to know the background which has led to this change. Here is a condensed version of the book of Genesis which is helpful for understanding God's new covenant. As mankind evolved and when the time was right, God selected one man, Abraham, to be the man through which he would bring salvation to the world. God made a covenant with Abraham and said to him; "Go forth from your country, and from your relatives and from your fathers house, to the land which I will show you; and I will make you a great nation, and I will bless you, and make your name great; and so you shall be a blessing; and I will bless those who bless you, and the one who curses you I will curse. And in you all the families of the earth will be blessed."

Abraham followed God and so became a great man for that time, and he had a son Isaac who also followed God and came to know him. Isaac became the father of Jacob who in like manner came to know God and to follow him. God changed Jacob's name to Israel and made the same covenant with Israel that had been made with his father and grandfather. Israel had twelve sons who became the patriarchs of the twelve tribes referred to by the name, "Hebrew" because they originated from Hebron in the land of Canaan. They and their descendants are also called the children of Israel. Of the twelve, Joseph was Israel's favorite and became the heir of the covenant, and was favored by God. What is important to remember is God's promise that through Abraham, all the families of the earth will be blessed.

PORK, BEEF, CHICKEN AND RIBS

Joseph's older brothers hated him because he was favored above them and finding an opportunity to dispose of him, sold him as a slave to some traders en route to Egypt. Joseph was sold as a slave to Potiphar, the captain of the bodyguard for Pharaoh. The Lord was with Joseph and he prospered in Egypt, and became known for his ability to interpret dreams through God, whom he served. Joseph interpreted Pharaoh's dream of a coming seven years of plenty, followed by seven years of famine; and so impressed the Pharaoh that he became the highest official in the land, and supervised the storage of grain during the good years and disbursement of it during the lean years, and he became famous in all of Egypt. The famine caused the children of Israel to seek relief from Egypt and they were reunited with Joseph; and in due course, came to live in Egypt. The Hebrew people who came to Egypt from Canaan numbered only about seventy-seven, and they prospered, and they multiplied in the land.

Throughout the years Joseph died and a new Pharaoh came to power that did not know him. Over time the Hebrews became slaves in Egypt. The Hebrews multiplied faster than did the Egyptians, and the Pharaoh became fearful that they would become great enough to overpower his people, so he declared that all male children born to the Hebrews were to be cast into the Nile. Now a man from the branch of Levi went and married a daughter of Levi. The woman conceived and bore a son who was so beautiful that she hid him for three months. When she could hide him no longer, she got a wicker basket and covered it over with tar and pitch so that it would float, and set it in the reeds along the bank of the Nile. His sister stood at a distance to find out what would happen to him. The daughter of Pharaoh came down to bathe, with her maidens walking alongside the Nile; and she saw the basket among the reeds and sent her maid, and she brought it to her. When she saw the baby she had pity on him. Then the sister of Moses who had been watching him said to Pharaoh's daughter, "Shall I go and call a nurse for you from the Hebrew women that she might nurse the child for you?" Pharaoh's daughter said, "go ahead." So the girl went and told their mother. Then Pharaoh's daughter said to her, "Take this child away and nurse him for me, and I will give you your wages." So the woman took the child and nursed him, and the child grew, and she brought him to Pharaoh's daughter and he became her adopted son, and she named him Moses.

Moses grew up in the household of the Pharaoh but with the knowledge that he was a Hebrew. When he was forty years old he saw an Egyptian mistreating a Hebrew man and was angry, and slew the Egyptian. When the Pharaoh heard of this he attempted to find Moses to kill him, but Moses escaped to the wilderness of Haran. There he made his life shepherding sheep; married; and had two sons with his wife Zipporah.

While he was keeping the sheep of Jetro, his father-in-law, he saw a bush on fire but the bush was not being consumed; and as he approached the bush God spoke to him. God made Moses the agent through whom he would free the Hebrew children from the bondage of the Egyptians. Moses was very reluctant, and insisted that his older brother Aaron be the speaker to communicate with Pharaoh, and God accepted. God brought many plagues upon Egypt in order to convince Pharaoh to release the Hebrews from captivity. He turned all the water in Egypt to blood, which caused all the fish in the Nile to die, and there was no water to drink. Pharaoh relented but when the water became normal he changed his mind. God brought plagues of frogs that came out of the Nile everywhere; even into the houses and the cooking pots, and finally Pharaoh relented and told Moses that he would let the people go. When the frogs were gone Pharaoh again changed his mind; and this was the pattern for five more devastating plagues of gnats, other insects, a severe pestilence upon the livestock of the Egyptians but not the Hebrews, a plague of boils on all the

PORK, BEEF, CHICKEN AND RIBS

Egyptians, and severe hail with thunder. For his eighth plague, God brought locust on an east wind that ate all the plants in Egypt and infiltrated their homes; until Pharaoh relented. Again he changed his mind. God then brought a deep darkness upon the land of Egypt; a darkness that could be felt, but Pharaoh would not relent and sent Moses away from him and directed that he was not to see the face of Moses again.

The tenth and final miracle which God performed in Egypt, he called the Passover. On a certain date, the fourteenth of the first month, God would send the angel of death to take the first born of every family in the land of Egypt, both man and beast. For protection from this plague it was necessary for the Hebrews to offer a sacrifice of a perfect lamb or goat of one year old, and to swab the blood of the sacrifice on the lintel and doorposts of the houses where they were staying.

At midnight the angel of death came through Egypt and took the life of all the first born children, except he would pass over the houses where he observed the blood of the sacrifice. It is important that the miracle of the Passover be known and understood because it demonstrates the saving of a life, or salvation, through faith. All of Egypt arose in the night with a great cry because there was not a household without someone dead. Then Pharaoh sent for Moses and Aaron at night and said to them, "Rise up, get out from among my people, both you and the sons of Israel; and go, worship the Lord, as you have said. Take both your flocks and your herds, as you have said, and go, and bless me also." The Egyptian people freely gave to the Hebrews their valuable possessions as gifts to God. There were six hundred thousand men in the Hebrew exodus out of Egypt along with their families and all their livestock. Now the time that the children of Israel lived in Egypt was 430 years, to the very day. God directed that the Hebrews were to celebrate the Passover each year, to remind them of that historic night in 1446

BC (Date is estimated). The exploits of Moses and the history of the flight of the Hebrew people from Egypt are recorded in the book of Exodus said to be written by Moses.

You have just read a summary of Genesis, the first book of the Bible. The stage is now set for you to understand how God's plan for the salvation of the world is to come about. Moses is credited with the writing of the book of Genesis from the traditional oral history passed down through the generations. He had been brought up as Pharaoh's grandson, and schooled to be literate, it is assumed. Moses is also credited with writing the books of Exodus, Leviticus, Numbers, and Deuteronomy, during the time of the exodus. These first five books of the Bible are referred to as the Pentateuch.

Following the Pentateuch, the books of the Old Testament take the names of their main characters or the writers. According to tradition, Samuel wrote the book of Judges, and probably most of Samuel after the death of Solomon in 930 BC. The two books of Samuel are actually a single literary work; and the same applies to 1 and 2 Kings, and 1 and 2 Chronicles. These are works of history and are not necessarily written during the period that is covered, and there is no definite proof establishing the writers. Beginning with Isaiah, the Bible takes on a more prophetic nature. Amos was the earliest of the books known as the *minor prophets* and was probably written 760–750 BC, followed shortly by Hosea. Joel might have been written before Amos and as early as 830 BC, but there is no datable historical event in the writing that establishes a date. Isaiah wrote from about 700 BC to 681 BC, and is considered to be the first writing prophet. His writings contain much of the prophecy of future events, which are contained in the Bible. Jeremiah follows Isaiah by a lifetime, and they are followed closely by Ezekiel. A number of minor prophets wrote in years following until Malachi who wrote 433–430 BC.

PORK, BEEF, CHICKEN AND RIBS

The first 40 chapters of Isaiah...From the forty first chapter Isaiah seems to move from a theme of Israel's failure to live up to God's expectations, to those "precious in his sight" who become his people under the new covenant. In Isaiah we are told in great detail about the coming prophet who will shepherd God's people Israel. We hear that God will form these people for himself and that they will have a new name. We learn the allegory/figurative name for the new prophet is God's own right hand or strong right arm and a grand new nation that all people will run too is envisioned, where foreigners will be the vinedressers and products from the whole world will flow to the new nation of Israel where justice will reign.

In the forty-third chapter we are told of a ransom agreement where God cedes several countries and their populations to the devil, in order to secure the well-being of the new Israel. This trade-off causes God to refer to himself as the "Redeemer," and this name is used in several other chapters of Isaiah, and other prophets in other books also call God "redeemer" because of this trade-off. This word is used in only two other contexts in the entire Bible; to describe redeeming the children of Israel from Pharaoh, and to refer to the promised Messiah the redeemer of the new Israel from their sins. Other prophets also foretell the changes that will occur in that day or at that time.

Through Moses, God taught the Hebrews what he required and what he desired, and they dutifully recorded that history for us and duplicated the scriptures for future generations. God proved himself to them with miracles that only he could perform as controller of nature. During the exodus, God began to tell Moses about a future change that would come about in the world that would not only encompass Israel but the entire world, and the spiritual world as well. This change was God's plan to bring you and all the inhabitants of the world into his plan for salvation. We refer to this historic change as the New Covenant, because

God had earlier made the covenant with Abraham which now must be referred to as the old covenant. Remember that God had been directly involved with only one family, descendants from Abraham, and the Old Testament scriptures are primarily a history of these people and their interaction with God.

There have been several significant changes in the activities of God and his relations to the physical world, which can be called turning points. The first of these is the exodus of the Hebrew children from slavery in Egypt. The ratification of the new covenant is the next and was definitely a major turning point in the interaction between God and the Spiritual realm, and mankind and the physical world. The third turning point was the Reformation. Europe awakened from the dark ages with a zeal for learning about God and for the first time in history information could be disseminated through the written word from the printing presses.

The beginning of the reformation was apparently the end of the famine for the word of God forecast by Amos, and also the end of the time allotted for Satan to control those nations given to him in the ransom agreement told about in Isaiah 43. I have purposely failed to refer to the coming of Christ as a turning point because the ratification of the new covenant at the time of the ransom agreement included the total interaction between good and evil that occurred as a result of his coming. The final turning point that will likely usher in the end of the age is the information age the Internet, a world wide web of knowledge. The information age places true and accurate knowledge of God before anyone with a computer, anywhere in the world. Even the Dead Sea Scrolls which proved the accuracy of our Bible are available for anyone to study on the Internet. The final prophesy says that the gospel will be preached to all people in the world before the day the Lord returns. Do you suspect the sermon will be in digital format?

PORK, BEEF, CHICKEN AND RIBS

THE NEW TESTAMENT

The New Testament was written by the disciples of Jesus, who was proven to be the righteous Branch by God himself, through miracles and revelations which were only possible through God. These miracles included healing the sick and the lame, casting out evil spirits, and restoring life to people who were dead. In addition, all the earlier predictions from the Old Testament prophets relating to the Messiah, were fulfilled in him. One other significant attribute of Jesus was that he could forgive people's sin. Only God can forgive sins. When Jesus told the paralytic (Luke 5:24) that his sins were forgiven, the scribes and Pharisees became enraged that Jesus would claim to be equal to God. The first four books of the New Testament were named for those disciples who wrote the narratives, and are referred to as the four gospels. The book of Acts is by Luke and continues his history of early Christianity. The most prolific writer of New Testament scriptures was Paul, selected by the resurrected Jesus to be his disciple to the gentiles. It is important that the selection of Paul be told about, and that will come later. Paul is the author of Romans and the following twelve books through Philemon.

The writer of the book of Hebrews is not firmly established, but the writings of the apostles James, Peter, and John, and a follower Jude complete the New Testament up to the last book, Revelation. The New Testament contains the history and teachings of Jesus, where you will find what you must do to gain God's salvation and take hold of the provisions of his new covenant; and these requirements are simple. You must believe that Jesus is who he claims to be and who God has proven him to be, and then you must publicly acknowledge this belief, and be baptized. In order to make an informed decision, you must learn of the Lord Jesus Christ, from some source or combination of sources. I give witness that the Bible is the word of God and the only true word. Avoid any religion that requires that you accept any other book in addition to the Bible, or in place of the Bible. The Holy Bible is the only true word of God, so read and study because the word is free, and it will make you free.

This saving grace of God was promised as a part of the new covenant by his promise; "I will forgive their iniquity, and their sin. I will remember no more." Provisions of the new covenant are told about in many places in the Old Testament scriptures and was first mentioned by God to Moses, when he said, "in those days I will raise up a prophet similar to you." Following this introduction by Moses there are many prophets in the Bible that tells of this promise by telling of the new covenant. The most recognized of these comes from Jeremiah. The new covenant was not made just for America and the western world but the entire human population known to us all over the world, and Jeremiah verifies this when he tells that the Righteous Branch will execute justice and righteousness on the earth.

> Behold, days are coming, declares the Lord, "when I will make a new covenant with the house of Israel and with the house of Judah, not like the covenant which I made with their fathers in the day I took them by the hand to bring them out of the land of Egypt, my Covenant which they broke, although I was a husband to them," declares the Lord. "But this is the covenant which I will make with the house of Israel after those days," declares the Lord, "I will put my law within them and on their heart I will write it; and I will be their God, and they shall be my people. "They will not teach again each man his neighbor and each man his brother, saying, 'Know the Lord,' for they will all know me, from the least of them to the greatest of them," declares the Lord, "for I will forgive their iniquity, and their sin I will remember no more.
>
> Jeremiah 31:31–34 (NASB)

God then gives his guarantee that this covenant will be forever, and he follows with some important additional information.

> Behold, days are coming," declares the Lord, "when I will fulfill the good word which I have spoken concerning the house of Israel and the house of Judah. In those days and at that time I will cause a righteous Branch of David to spring forth; and he shall execute justice and righteousness on the earth. In those days Judah will be saved and Jerusalem will dwell in safety; and this is the name by which she will be called: 'the Lord is our righteousness.'
>
> Jeremiah 33:14–16 (NASB)

The similar guarantee is then repeated that followed the promise in Jeremiah 31:34. If you can break my covenant for the day and my covenant for the night, so that day and night will not be at their appointed time, then my covenant may also be broken with David my servant (Jeremiah 33:20—21, NASB).

This good word given to us by the Almighty God, is the grandest news to ever be told to mankind and was told to us about two thousand six hundred years ago. This righteous Branch of David forecast by Jeremiah, was brought forth in the person of Jesus Christ in Bethlehem, with the birth of a child proclaimed to be the Son of the Most High, as the prophets had forecast. When he was about twenty-seven years of age, he began to preach repentance for sins, and to teach the ways of God. John, the son of Zacharias, had begun to preach repentance prior to Jesus, and would baptize the people as a symbolic gesture to wash away their sins. John also foretold of one coming after him who was greater than him and identified Jesus as "The Lamb of God." Zacharias, the father of John the Baptist, filled with the Holy Spirit, had prophesied when he was born, saying:

And you, child, will be called the prophet of the Most High; for you will go on before the Lord to prepare his ways; to give to his people the knowledge of salvation by the forgiveness of their sins, because of the tender mercy of our God, with which the Sunrise from on high will visit us, to shine upon those who sit in darkness and the shadow of death, to guide our feet into the way of peace." And the child continued to grow and to become strong in spirit, and he lived in the deserts until the day of his public appearance to Israel.

Luke 1:76 –80 (NASB)

After Jesus had come to be baptized by John the Baptist, John began to tell about Jesus, and what had been revealed to him from God the Father. The story of Jesus being baptized by John comes from Matthew, and from the disciple John.

(John the baptist speaking) "As for me, I baptize you with water for repentance, but he who is coming after me is mightier than I, and I am not fit to remove his sandals; he will baptize you with the Holy Spirit and fire. His winnowing fork is in his hand, and he will thoroughly clear his threshing floor; and he will gather his wheat into the barn, but he will burn up the chaff with unquenchable fire." Then Jesus arrived from Galilee at the Jordan coming to John, to be baptized by him. But John tried to prevent him, saying, "I have need to be baptized by you, and do you come to me?" But Jesus answering said to him, "Permit it at this time; for in this way it is fitting for us to fulfill all righteousness." Then he permitted him. After being baptized, Jesus came up immediately from the water; and behold, the heavens were opened, and he saw the Spirit of God descending as a dove and lighting on him, and behold, a voice out of the heavens said, "This is my beloved Son, in whom I am well-pleased.

Matthew 3:11–17 (NASB)

PORK, BEEF, CHICKEN AND RIBS

> The next day he (John the Baptist) saw Jesus coming to him and said," Behold, the lamb of God who takes away the sin of the world! This is he on behalf of whom I said, 'After me comes a man who has a higher rank than I, for he existed before me.' I did not recognize him, but so that he might be manifested to Israel, I came baptizing in water." John testified saying, "I have seen the Spirit descending as a dove out of heaven, and he remained upon him. I did not recognize him, but he who sent me to baptize in water said to me, 'he upon whom you see the Spirit descending and remaining upon him, this is the one who baptizes in the Holy Spirit.' I myself have seen, and have testified that this is the Son of God." Again the next day John was standing with two of his disciples, and he looked at Jesus as he walked, and said, "Behold, the Lamb of God!" The two disciples heard him speak, and they followed Jesus.
>
> John 1:29–37 (NASB)

After his baptism Jesus was ready to begin his ministry, and began to preach repentance from sin, and embraced John's practice of baptism to spiritually wash away those sins from which you have repented. Jesus continued his teaching about God for more than a year and became famous because he did things that only God can do. He healed the sick. He miraculously restored the eyes of people born blind, and the limbs of people born lame. He would exorcise evil spirits that affected the minds of those afflicted. He raised people who were dead, back to life. Lazarus, whom he raised from death, had been dead for four days which prompted his sister Martha to say, "But Lord there will be a stench, for he has been dead four days." The miracles which Jesus performed and his teachings about what is right for us, were recorded by his disciples and are available to us today in the New Testament portion of the Bible. He magnified two fish and five loaves of bread into enough to feed five thousand people who had followed him until they were hungry. Just imagine the interest generated in the area where he preached. The established leaders of the Jews, refused to accept that Jesus was the Messiah, and because of their unbelief caused his death by crucifixion. God's covenant is this: God, the Almighty, wants to offer you salvation, and life everlasting, through his love for you expressed in the person of his Son, Jesus Christ, and the Branch of David, who became the willing sacrifice on the cross at Calvary, to atone for the sins of the world. This was God's idea. It is his plan from the beginning, and there was no input from any human mind that influenced his decision. This statement must be emphasized! The plan for salvation of mankind is God's plan and only his. Mankind must only believe God and accept his plan.

THE REQUIREMENTS FOR SALVATION

What are the requirements for you to go to heaven when your life on earth is finished? God does not obscure his plan, but makes it very plain and very simple, to the extent that many people cannot accept it. Jesus Christ, who was God in the flesh, was made a sacrifice for the sins of the world, and he was sacrificed on the cross, was dead and buried; and the third day he rose from the dead; and now is alive and sits by the Father in heaven. The Holy Spirit was provided to the Christian believers following his ascension into heaven, and we are saved through faith in him, and receive the Holy Spirit upon profession of that faith, and baptism in his name. The only requirement to join in the covenant relationship with God, the All Mighty God, Yhwy, the God of the Bible by any name, is to believe in his Son, the Messiah who he told Moses about some one thousand four hundred years before the Son was born. The most popular verse in the New Testament, confirms this requirement.

PORK, BEEF, CHICKEN AND RIBS

> For God so loved the world that he gave his only begotten Son, that whoever believes in him shall not perish, but have eternal life.
>
> John 3:16 (NASB)

How can this be? In Isaiah 54:9, a promise was made by God when he said: "So I have sworn that I will not be angry with you, nor will I rebuke you." Once we join in his covenant he will not get angry regardless of what we do. That is his promise; nor will he punish us for anything. How can this be? There were no requirements attached to his promise other than you must believe on the Son, and this faith makes you a party to his covenant. The answer to this fantastic relationship with God is simply this: he has given all authority to Jesus, and Jesus tells us this.

> "All authority has been given to me in heaven and on earth. Go therefore and make disciples of all the nations, baptizing them in the name of the Father and the Son and the Holy Spirit, teaching them to observe all that I commanded you; and lo, I am with you always, even to the end of the age."
>
> Matthew 28: 18–20 (NASB)

> Truly, truly, I say to you, he who hears my Word, and believes him who sent me, has eternal life, and does not come into judgment, but has passed out of death into life.
>
> John 5:24 (NASB)

Before his crucifixion, Jesus told his disciples about his coming death and that he would rise again on the third day, and they did not understand. He told them that he must be lifted up like Moses lifted up the serpent in the wilderness, and they did not understand. It was after his resurrection when he opened their understanding of what had been forecast about him in the prophets and the Psalms, that they began to understand the significance of the crucifixion and resurrection. In keeping with God's promise, "I will forgive their iniquity, and their sin I will remember no more", for us to gain salvation we need only believe that Jesus Christ is the Son of God. There is no requirement for us to say anything or eat anything or to refrain from eating anything. It is not required for us to go anywhere, or perform any feat or run any race, or to even face a certain direction. Believe in Jesus Christ and you shall be saved. That is much too easy for many people to accept or believe, but John, the brother of James and son of Zebedee, and a disciple of Jesus, reports the following words from Jesus.

> For God so loved the world, that he gave his only begotten Son, that whoever believes in him shall not perish, but have eternal life." "For God did not send his Son into the world to judge the world, but that the world might be saved through him." "He who believes in him is not judged; he who does not believe has been judged already, because he has not believed in the name of the only begotten Son of God."
>
> John 3:16-18 (NASB)

This is the only requirement for a person to take hold of the new covenant provided by the Almighty God for their salvation; believe that Jesus is the only begotten Son of God. God grants salvation to anyone who believes in Jesus Christ; or in other words, God grants eternal life to anyone who loves Jesus. This was the grandest news to ever be told, and the disciples of Jesus told it well and many people believed. Many Christian denominations believe that when a person believes, then they must so pronounce that belief and be baptized. This baptism signifies that a person is dead in Christ from sin, and then being raised to a new life with Christ without sin. This ritual cleansing and becoming a new person is referred to as being born again. Does this make us free from sin? No, everyone is guilty of sin in some way, so it becomes necessary for the Christian believer to ask forgiveness in prayer. There is a promise from God that he will forgive our sins and cleanse us from all unrighteousness.

> This is the message we have heard from him and announce to you, that God is Light, and in him there is no darkness at all. If we say that we have fellowship with him and yet walk in the darkness, we lie and do not practice the truth; but if we walk in the Light as he himself is in the Light, we have fellowship with one another, and the blood of Jesus his Son cleanses us from all sin. If we say that we have no sin, we are deceiving ourselves and the truth is not in us. If we confess our sins, he is faithful and righteous to forgive us our sins and to cleanse us from all unrighteousness.
>
> 1 John 1: 5–10 (NASB)

God does not place a limit on the number of sins he will forgive; and remember, God looks into the heart of those who seek him. It is very important that anyone seeking to know God recognizes that he is holy, and must be respected in order to be reached. God said in Leviticus 10:3: "by those who come near me, I will be treated holy." This is a mandatory requirement. If you do not have a reverence for God, you will never be able to communicate with him. Christianity assumes that it is the only religion which will be successful in providing salvation to its adherents, and the entire Bible supports this assumption. There is no plan for salvation of the human race except by way of the new covenant that God has made with the worlds. It is very important that you realize this fact. If there were another way, God would have told us about it in the Bible. The Apostle Peter makes this very clear.

> And there is salvation in no one else; for there is no other name under heaven that has been given among men by which we must be saved.
>
> Acts 4:12 (NASB)

The salvation which God provided for us through the sacrifice of his Son on the cross was explained by the Apostle Paul, so that the world can understand that *Faith* in Jesus Christ is the determining factor that God desires in us. The Apostle Paul has put into proper words the fact that we are saved by faith in Jesus Christ to save us from any form of punishment in the afterlife. Paul holds that under the dispensation of grace, we are not obligated or expected to fulfill the requirements of the moral law in order to gain our salvation. Paul bases this antinomian theology on what Jesus has said about the subject of believing that he came as the Son of God to be the sacrifice that covers our transgressions.

> Therefore, everyone who confesses me before men, I will also confess him before my Father who is in heaven. But whoever denies me before men, I will also deny him before my Father who is in heaven.
>
> Matthew 10:32–33 (NASB)

> Therefore there is now no condemnation for those who are in Christ Jesus. For the law of the Spirit of life in Christ Jesus has set you free from the law of sin and of death. For what the Law could not do, weak as it was through the flesh, God did: sending his own Son in the likeness of sinful flesh and as an offering for sin, he condemned sin in the flesh, so that the requirement of the Law might be fulfilled in us, who do not walk according to the flesh but according to the Spirit. For those who are according to the flesh set their minds on the things of the flesh, but those who are according to the Spirit, the things of the Spirit.

PORK, BEEF, CHICKEN AND RIBS

For the mind set on the flesh is death, but the mind set on the Spirit is life and peace, because the mind set on the flesh is hostile toward God; for it does not subject itself to the law of God, for it is not even able to do so, and those who are in the flesh cannot please God. However, you are not in the flesh but in the Spirit, if indeed the Spirit of God dwells in you. But if anyone does not have the Spirit of Christ, he does not belong to him.

Romans 8: 1–9 (NASB)

But thanks be to God that though you were slaves of sin, you became obedient from the heart to that form of teaching to which you were committed, and having been freed from sin, you became slaves of righteousness. I am speaking in human terms because of the weakness of your flesh. For just as you presented your members as slaves to impurity and to lawlessness, resulting in further lawlessness, so now present your members as slaves to righteousness, resulting in sanctification. For when you were slaves of sin, you were free in regard to righteousness. Therefore what benefit were you then deriving from the things of which you are now ashamed? For the outcome of those things is death. But now having been freed from sin and enslaved to God, you derive your benefit, resulting in sanctification, and the outcome, eternal life. For the wages of sin is death, but the free gift of God is eternal life in Christ Jesus our Lord.

Romans 6:17–23 (NASB)

Therefore, having been justified by faith, we have peace with God through our Lord Jesus Christ, through whom also we have obtained our introduction by faith into this grace in which we stand; and we exult in hope of the glory of God. And not only this, but we also exult in our tribulations, knowing that tribulation brings about perseverance; and perseverance, proven character; and proven character, hope; and hope does not disappoint, because the love of God has been poured out within our hearts through the Holy Spirit who was given to us. For while we were still helpless, at the right time, Christ died for the ungodly. For one will hardly die for a righteous man; though perhaps for the good man someone would dare even to die. But God demonstrates his own love toward us, in that while we were yet sinners, Christ died for us. Much more then, having now been justified by his blood, we shall be saved from the wrath of God through him.

Romans 5:1–9 (NASB)

The background of the Christian faith is the theology put forth by the Apostle Paul who was taught it from God. Paul is accepted as more authoritative because he was selected by the risen Christ to be his disciple, taught by him, and then shown inexpressible visions that would occur at future times. The Apostle Paul received communication from God comparable to that of Moses.

Come to me, all who are weary and heavy-laden, and I will give you rest. "Take my yoke upon you and learn from me, for I am gentle and humble in heart, and you will find rest for your souls. "For my yoke is easy and My burden is light."

Matthew 11:28–30 (NASB)

These are words from Jesus inviting all who will to come to him for salvation, and his promise is that life will be easy and his burden placed on you will be light, and in truth it is a joy. From somewhere I copied these words: "God's word is always valid without reference to its original context—A living Word." (close is Hebrews 4:12–13. 1 Thessalonians 2:13, Romans 10:8–

11, 17) The Apostle Peter gives an explanation of the prophets writing in times past, of things that would happen in later years. The Living Bible, paraphrased, gives the best interpretation of Peter's statement:

> This salvation was something the prophets did not fully understand. Though they wrote about it, they had many questions as to what it all could mean. They wondered what the Spirit of Christ within them was talking about, for he told them to write down the events which, since then, have happened to Christ: his suffering and his great glory afterwards. And they wondered when and to whom all this would happen. They were finally told that these things would not occur during their lifetime, but long years later, during yours. And now at last this Good News has been plainly announced to all of us. It was preached to us in the power of the same heaven-sent Holy Spirit who spoke to them; and it is all so strange and wonderful that even the angels in heaven would give a great deal to know more about it.
>
> 1 Peter 1:10–12 The Living Bible Paraphrased

PROMISES FROM GOD

Throughout the Bible, God makes promises that affect us and it is important to know these promises. The most important promise made by him is the promise that he will never change. By this promise you can be assured that when you enter into a relationship with God, that relationship will never change by anything coming from him. You can trust him. He plainly tells us that he does not change in many scriptures. Following the ransom in Isaiah he tells several times that he is the only god, and in Isaiah 44:6 and 48:12 that he is the last.

God would know that Satan would present himself as god in a religion organized in that part of the world ceded to him in the ransom; hence the strong messages to alert us to the fact that he would not change. Satan was envious of God and wanted to be worshipped, and it was that desire which caused him to agree with the terms of the new covenant. Because God does not change, we can know with certainty that he is not the God of the Koran. God is not finished with humankind because he is still evolving our relationship with himself. Plans, which he has made and told about through the prophets, are still unfolding before the world. Before the present Christian era, God was committed to only one nation, Israel, the descendants of Abraham. When he decided the time was right, he set in motion a much expected new covenant with mankind, which includes everyone in the whole world. God has the authority to make a new covenant with us. He can do that. We can only agree with this contract and accept it, or we can reject it. The heart of the new covenant is Jesus Christ our Lord. Read God's promise concerning his Savior:

> Behold, my Servant whom I uphold; my chosen one in whom my soul delights. I have put my Spirit upon him; he will bring forth justice to the nations. He will not cry out or raise his voice, nor make his voice heard in the street. A bruised reed he will not break and a dimly burning wick he will not extinguish; he will faithfully bring forth justice. He will not be disheartened or crushed until he has established justice in the earth and the coastlands will wait expectantly for his law. Thus, says God the Lord, Who created the heavens and stretched them out, who spread out the earth and its offspring, who gives breath to the people on it and spirit to those who walk in it, I am the Lord, I have called you in righteousness, I will also hold you by the hand and watch over you, and I will appoint you as a covenant to the people, as a light to the nations, to open blind eyes, to bring out prisoners from the dungeon and those who dwell in darkness from the prison. I am the

Lord, that is my name; I will not give my glory to another, nor my praise to graven images. Behold the former things have come to pass, now I declare new things; before they spring forth, I proclaim them to you.

Isaiah 42:1–9 (NASB)

The testimony from Isaiah:

For a child will be born to us, a son will be given to us; And the government will rest on his shoulders; And his name will be called Wonderful Counselor, Mighty God, Eternal Father, Prince of Peace. There will be no end to the increase of his government or of peace, on the throne of David and over his kingdom, to establish it and to uphold it with justice and righteousness from then on and forevermore. The zeal of the Lord of host will accomplish this.

Isaiah 9:6–7 (NASB)

The testimony of Jesus.

As Moses lifted up the serpent in the wilderness, even so must the Son of Man be lifted up; so that whoever believes will in him have eternal life. For God so loved the world, that he gave his only begotten Son, that whoever believes in him shall not perish, but have eternal life. For God did not send the Son into the world to judge the world, but that the world might be saved through him. He who believes in him is not judged; he who does not believe has been judged already, because he has not believed in the name of the only begotten Son of God.

John 3:14–8 (NASB)

The testimony of John the Baptist.

> He who comes from above is above all; he who is of the earth is from the earth and speaks of the earth. He who comes from heaven is above all. What he has seen and heard, of that he testifies; and no one receives his testimony. He who has received his testimony has set his seal to this, that God is true. For he whom God has sent speaks the words of God; for he gives the Spirit without measure. The Father loves the Son and has given all things into his hand. He who believes in the Son has eternal life; but he who does not obey the Son will not see life, but the wrath of God abides on him.
>
> John 3:31–36 (NASB)

John the Baptist was the last prophet of God and this is verified by Jesus at Matthew 11:13. Many pagan gods were worshipped in the time of Paul, and these are evident in Athens as described in Acts chapter 16, and Artemis, pagan god of the Ephesians is famous from Chapter 19 of Acts. The end of evil spirits affecting the lives of human beings began with Christ, and the New Testament records many examples of evil spirits being exorcized by Jesus and his followers. When you study the Bible, look for other instances of spiritual involvement prior to Christ, and of other changes that were brought about with his coming. Christianity and Islam have eliminated the worship of pagan gods and their names can only be found through study of history or from ancient statuary that has been preserved from those days.

A very important promise for all mankind is that if you will draw closer to God then he will draw closer to you. This promise carries the requirement that you must initiate any relationship with him, but it also carries the guarantee that you will not fail to get his attention.

THE TRINITY

The subject of the Trinity must be discussed and hopefully understood. There is no separation between God the Father, Jesus the Son, and the Holy Spirit. The Trinity is not a result of any man-made conference or theological teaching, but is a normal definition of the heavenly beings that come with the new covenant from God, the Father. We know from Moses that mankind cannot look upon God the Almighty without being harmed, and recall the fear of the people when God spoke directly to them at Horeb.

God in a human form was desired so that people could look upon him, learn from his mouth, and become witnesses to the greatness of God; therefore, God chooses the Virgin Mary to bear and to give birth to his only begotten son, and named him Jesus. He was not selected from the population as Moses was but born naturally through human birth, and matured naturally from infant to manhood, and he followed the teachings of the elders of the Hebrew nation which was his birthright.

The moment of Christ's death, as a human being free from sin, was the moment in time that the devil was defeated, and cast down from heaven. That was the moment in time when the new covenant was sealed within the universe. God has told us about the covenant and many of the provisions of it, but the devil would have tried to defeat God's plan to the very end, and his victory could have been determined by a simple complaint from the mouth of Jesus. The twenty second Psalm appears to be the recorded mind of Jesus as he suffered on the cross. If that interpretation is correct, then it is apparent that every utterance from Christ on the cross is respectful to God the Father. It was at his death that the veil of the temple was torn apart from top to bottom, and the "Holy of Holies", that area of the temple that was previously seen only by the priest, was now accessible to the common man. This was the signal of victory for all humanity.

There is no god but him. There are many examples in the Old Testament scripture where God teaches us that there are no other gods. A very poignant scripture in my opinion is where Moses asked to see God, and God wants to show himself to Moses, but no human can survive the impact of seeing the God Almighty. Understand that Moses is one of the few humans that God could speak with "face to face," and God naturally loves Moses and was attempting to show himself to Moses without injuring him, and had him hide in the rocks until he had passed by and then to look upon his backside. It is from this episode that we learned that no man can look upon God the Almighty and live.

I find the idea that God should send his son in human form, which we can see without any problem, to be a logical means for God to show himself to us. There is no conflict between the three manifestations of God, and the Trinity is not a man-made determination of God's body makeup. How do we know about the Holy Spirit? We were told about him by Jesus, and then we were shown him at Pentecost. I also see the dedication of the Holy Spirit upon a Christian as a logical way to accomplish the writing of his law on our hearts as promised by the covenant. I know that he is present because I have responded to his leading and have heard his voice.

God is real. I have learned this through prayer and having received answer to prayer. Here are three notable examples that are easy for me to relate to you. I had started smoking at an early age because I thought it was the "thing" to do. I was addicted and I was unable to stop smoking cigarettes until I asked God for his help. Each time that I put a cigarette in my mouth and put the lighter in my hand, I would hesitate before lighting the cigarette and silently ask God to take away my desire to smoke. The desire would go away just as though I had smoked the cigarette. I had smoked a pack of cigarettes each day for over 30 years so that short prayer was answered about twenty times each day. It was three months before I felt comfortable enough to stop carrying the cigarettes and lighter. Never did the desire to smoke fail to leave me immediately after asking God to take it away, and the most significant result was relief from my craving as though I had smoked the cigarette.

My next example was in 1992. I had taken a job to prepare a large sixty thousand gallon propane tank for shipping and to supervise moving the tank from behind a matching tank which was filled with gas. The job was complicated by the location of the tanks on the side of a hill, and the customer wanted the front tank to remain in place. Prior to starting the job I asked God to keep anyone from being hurt and to keep me from doing anything that would ruin my reputation. The first day I worked alone and evacuated the propane gas vapor from the rear tank and filled it with nitrogen vapor. All of this I had done hundreds of times and was routine to my job. I was cutting the three connecting pipe between the two tanks with an abrasive saw, believing the pipe to be filled with inert nitrogen, and while cutting into the last pipe, someone said to me; "stop cutting." As I raised the saw from the pipe, a small stream of liquid propane began to spew from the cut I had made. My response was to immediately shut off the engine of the saw and retreat from the gas, and then I turned to see who had spoken to me. There was no one there, and I said, "Thank you, Lord." The instruction to stop cutting the pipe was an audible sound, and I heard this sound in my ear. When I saw that no person was behind me to make the sound, I knew that it was God that had warned me.

My third example of answered prayer happened on a vacation trip with our friends, whom I will name Richard and Faye for their privacy. Before leaving their driveway, I asked Richard to pray for a safe trip because I felt it necessary. After an uneventful trip to Hilton Head, SC, and during an excursion to Daufuskie Island, my wife saw Faye begin to climb the boarding steps to board the ferry, and I heard her say, "Catch Faye" So I rushed to a position to catch her (she is bothered by Parkinson's disease). As I barely reached a position to catch her, she fell backward, safely into my arms. Had I not been there, Faye would have fallen to the dock with one leg caught between the boat and the three boarding steps. I later asked my wife how she knew Faye would fall and learned that she had said "Be ready to catch Faye." If I had heard her correctly, I might not have hurried so fast. Prayer for protection seems to focus God's attention to your dependence upon him. I know that I would have started a fire without his intervention in 1992, and I suspect that he would not have intervened if I had not invited him by prayer to do so.

These three examples of answered prayer are only three of hundreds which were just as positive in God's response but more difficult to describe. The way to prove that God is real is to seek to know him, and that means trying to interact with him by simply talking with him in prayer. One of God's promises is that if you draw closer to him, he will draw closer to you. Notice that promise and read it again—if you draw closer to him, he will draw closer to you.

The important thing is that you must make the first move, for God will not intervene into your conscious world without invitation. When you invite God into your life, do not expect an earthshaking response from him. God does not give you a more intelligent mind, when you choose to follow his way. There is no drastic exciting change in your everyday existence. The subtle changes are best seen over time by looking back at the changes in your life. The most noticeable change for me was the realization that I felt love for other believers. I also thought that I could ascertain the sincere believer from those who only wanted a donation, and I still feel that I can do that. God does not change.

This is important to know because when you begin to seek him, you already know that he will draw closer to you, because he has made that promise.

I have no difficulty believing in the Trinity; however, when the Holy Spirit stopped me from cutting into the propane-filled pipe, I called him God. And it makes no difference. The warning came from God the Father through the Holy Spirit or Comforter promised by God and instituted at Pentecost. We know that the Holy Spirit comes to a person after being saved in the name of the Lord Jesus. We know this from Paul and Apollos through Acts 19, when they re-baptized the twelve disciples who had only received John's baptism of repentance. By requiring the name of Jesus, does this make him a different entity from the Father? Perhaps it does but *it* makes no difference. Think of God the Almighty, Jesus Christ our Lord, and the Holy Spirit as being like the inner workings of my computer with millions of pieces of information stored within its memory chips and hard drive; does it matter which causes the computer to react, when the action is always the same? There can be no difference of thought or action between the three; because they are all in unison—they are all one.

The author of the Koran wants everyone to think that the Trinity is three separate beings with different agenda, but this is false. The mind of God is the mind of Jesus and the Holy Spirit is of the same thoughts. Competition between them is not possible. Jesus explained that he and the father are one (John 10:30 NASB).

THE HOLY SPIRIT

The Holy Spirit was first promised in conjunction with the new covenant from God in Jer. 31:31 –34. It was said that he would write his law on our heart, and that he would forgive our sins, and that we would be his people and he would be our God. This was to occur at some time in the future, and involve the remnant of Israel whom God was to redeem from the hand of him who was stronger than them (Jer. 31:11). We then learn in chapter 33 that a Righteous Branch from the root of Jessie would spring forth to bring this new covenant to fruition. The people so redeemed and who hold God's law in their hearts are described in Isaiah 43:4 as precious in God's sight. An interesting record of the Holy Spirit is when Peter was reporting to the brethren in Jerusalem about the conversion of Cornelius and his household, and how the Holy Spirit was poured out on them.

Peter said: "And I remember the word of the Lord, how he used to say, 'John baptized with water, but you will be baptized with the Holy Spirit.'" "From this report, the Lord apparently told of the Holy Spirit many times and there is, of course, many other reports of that. John the Baptist first told of the Holy Spirit when he told about Jesus in Matthew 3:11: "As for me, I baptize you with water for repentance; but he who is coming after me is mightier than I, and I am not fit to remove his sandals; he will baptize you with the Holy Spirit and with fire." I interpret "and with fire" to mean the refining process which Christians are subjected to. The requirement to be a Christian is to believe in Jesus, that he was the Son of God, and that he was crucified as a sacrifice for our sins, and that he ascended to heaven and abides now with God the Father; and it is this faith that places our welfare into the hands of Jesus Christ that makes us one of the multitude of Christians.

The John writes: John 1:11–13 (NASB) which says, "He (Christ) came to his own, and those who were his own (the Jews) did not receive him. But as many as received him (Christians), to them he gave the right to become children of God, even to those who believe in his name, who were born, not of blood nor of the will of the flesh nor of the will of man, but of God."

This new birth was explained to Nicodemus, by Jesus, as the need to be born of the spirit. This new birth of the spirit, within those who believe God, is the fulfillment of the new covenant God has made with all humankind, and there is no distinction between Jew and Greek, rich and poor, male and female, or slave and free. Jesus verified this "new birth."

> Truly, truly, I say to you, he who hears my Word, and believes him who sent me, has eternal life, and does not come into judgment, but has passed out of death into life.
>
> John 5:24 (NASB)

Every Christian receives the gift of the Holy Spirit, although it may not be as noticeable as at the first times when the recipient would speak in tongues. At my conversion the most obvious indication of the Holy Spirit was a feeling of love for other Christians, and then came the ability to discern the sincerity of another regarding their Christianity. There is a marked difference between a true Christian and a person who does not possess this gift of the Holy Spirit. It is the Holy Spirit that quietly urges us to take a certain path, or to read a particular book, or select our profession, or the church group that we will join. It is the Holy Spirit that gives us an urging to tell others of our faith, as Isaiah wrote for God: "The people whom I formed for myself will declare my praise" (Isa. 43:21 NASB).

God has promised that he will forgive our sins, and promised us everlasting life, and rest for our souls. A Christian needs not fear the judgment which all others must attend, for God has exempted us from the judgment because of our trust in Jesus to save our souls from death; therefore, when our bodies die, our soul lives. This is why Jesus said that whoever believes in him has passed from death unto life, and what he meant when he told his listeners that there were some among them that would not die until they saw him coming in his glory. When our physical bodies die, our soul will enter into God's rest, just like Daniel who was informed of his rest in the last verse of the book of Daniel.

> But as for you, (Daniel) go your way to the end; then you will enter into rest and rise again for your allotted portion at the end of the age.
>
> Daniel 12:13 (NASB)

You must also understand that there is a spiritual realm which cannot be seen as we see the physical world. God proves this spiritual realm to those who believe in him in various ways, the most prevalent is by answering prayer. If you do not seek God's assistance through prayer, then you do not give him the chance to prove himself to you; therefore, prayer is a necessary activity in the life of a Christian. Jesus taught us to go to the Father in prayer in order to seek his guidance, and there are several examples in the Bible of prayer being answered.

King Hezekiah prayed fervently to God for his life after Samuel told him of God's plan to take his life, and God changed his mind and gave Hezekiah fifteen more years of life. This is the best example demonstrating the effectiveness of prayer and from it we learn that God will sometimes change his mind; however, his character does not change and he tells this many times throughout the scriptures. Another example of God changing his mind is told in Jonah because Nineveh repented because of Jonah's preaching and God changed his mind about destroying the city.

Now you know many of the teachings of the Bible and you have read of the most marvelous news to ever be proclaimed and that is the salvation of our souls through faith in Jesus Christ. The entire work of the prophets; the entire teachings of God culminate with the salvation of your soul, the everlasting pleasure to be provided you in the afterlife. I know how it feels to be in heaven with the Lord, and it is inexpressible joy when God wraps you in his love, every fiber in your body reacts with joy. Happiness overwhelms you.

JOY THE PROOF OF OUR SALVATION

I believe that we are living in the days of the great tribulation, but Christians will go out with joy and be led forth with peace. One trait that is evident above all others among my fellow Christians is a feeling of joy —Joy for just being alive, and even more joy if they enjoy good health. This joy is magnified when a group of similarly-minded people convene. This joy is lacking from other religions, which teach that good deeds determine salvation, for a person is never sure that they have done enough good or not. It is for sure that many other religions produce good people, but Christianity is the only religion which I have studied, in which God provides a sure method that allows us to know that our salvation is assured. That assurance comes from our own mind because of our faith in our Savior Jesus Christ, who is the Branch of David that was sent by God the Almighty to redeem all who believe in him. This is the word of faith that says (Rom. 10:9 NASB) "if you confess with your mouth Jesus as Lord, and believe in your heart that God has raised him from the dead, you will be saved." This is God's plan, and there was no other input from any other source. The apostle Peter tells that this joy which he described as, "joy inexpressible," is the proof of our salvation.

> Blessed be the God and Father of our Lord Jesus Christ, who according to his great mercy has caused us to be born again to a living hope through the resurrection of Jesus Christ from the dead, to obtain an inheritance which is imperishable and undefiled and will not fade away, reserved in heaven for you, who are protected by the power

of God through faith for a salvation ready to be revealed in the last time.

In this you greatly rejoice, even though now for a little while, if necessary, you have been distressed by various trials, so that the proof of your faith, being more precious than gold which is perishable, even though tested by fire, may be found to result in praise and glory and honor at the revelation of Jesus Christ; and though you have not seen him, you love him, and though you do not see him now, but believe in him, you greatly rejoice with joy inexpressible and full of glory, obtaining as the outcome of your faith the salvation of your souls.

As to this salvation, the prophets who prophesied of the grace that would come to you made careful searches and inquiries, seeking to know what person or time the Spirit of Christ within them was indicating as he predicted the sufferings of Christ and the glories to follow. It was revealed to them that they were not serving themselves, but you, in these things which now have been announced to you through those who preached the gospel to you by the Holy Spirit sent from heaven—things into which angels long to look.

1 Peter 1:3–12 (NASB)

There are important prophesies that I find interconnected to reveal the plans that God has made for this universe. First, when he called me to follow his plan for salvation, he gave me the feeling of being wrapped in his love which I perceive is what it is like to be in heaven. Then as I began to seriously study in order to make myself approved by God, I was afforded an understanding of the scriptures that made me recognize his plan. Now, it is necessary for me to write this treatise. During the Exodus, God began to reveal his plan through Moses. Then through the Prophet Amos he reveals that only a third of humanity will become his people, and that they will dwell in their own land, and also that he will test them in their dedication to him. Amos also revealed that there would be a time that his word would not be available to the people, and calls that, "a famine for the word of God."

Through the Prophets Isaiah and Jeremiah, God expands on his plan for a new covenant, and reveals that this new covenant will be for the whole world, and will result in salvation for his people, and be ushered in by a descendant of David. Through most of the prophets, other changes to occur because of his new covenant are revealed which are centered on changes to take place in the relationship between the world we know and the spiritual world. The forecast was for an end to the prophets, fortune-tellers, diviners, and soothsayers and denotes a definite increase in separation between the physical world and the spiritual. Then in an unusual move, God tells of paying a ransom in order to secure the provisions of his new covenant, and calls himself "Redeemer" by virtue of that transaction.

Prophesy then slows until the Apostles of the one sent to usher in the new covenant begin to reveal what will occur at a later time. The Apostle Paul makes the most astounding of these by telling of the apostasy that must occur before the end time, and warns of the force perpetrating the apostasy. Secular history reveals the force that renounces God's plan for our salvation. The purpose of this treatise is to inform God's people of that force.

THE APOSTLE PAUL

The Apostle Paul was the most important of the apostles of Christ because he was chosen by our risen Lord, and designated as the apostle for the gentiles. Paul tells of being taken up into heaven and seeing inexpressible visions and of being taught by the Lord himself rather that gaining his knowledge of Gods teachings from men. Apparently the Christians in Thessalonica were disrupting their lives because they were expecting an eminent return of the Lord Jesus. In order to set their minds at ease, Paul revealed to them that the Lord would not return until after an apostasy had occurred, and then gives some detailed information of the apostasy. This prophesy is the most important revelation made by the Apostle Paul. There are other places in the Bible where Paul tells of things that must occur, and he usually testifies that what he says to us is from the Lord. If he gives us a teaching that is not given to him from the Lord, he will so indicate that what he is saying is from his own mind. This testimony from Paul is his greatest teaching relating to the return of the Lord.

> Now we request you, brethren, with regard to the coming of our Lord Jesus Christ and our gathering together to him, that you not be quickly shaken from your composure or be disturbed either by a spirit or message or a letter as if from us, to the effect that the day of the Lord has come. Let no

one in any way deceive you, for it will not come unless the apostasy comes first, and the man of lawlessness is revealed, the son of destruction, who opposes and exalts himself above every so-called god or object of worship, so that he takes his seat in the temple of God, displaying himself as being God.

Do you not remember that while I was still with you, I was telling you these things? And you know what restrains him now, so that in his time he will be revealed. For the mystery of lawlessness is already at work; only he who now restrains will do so until he is taken out of the way.

Then that lawless one will be revealed whom the Lord will slay with the breath of his mouth and bring to an end by the appearance of his coming; that is, the one whose coming in accord with the activity of Satan, with all power and signs and false wonders, and with all the deception of the wickedness for those who perish, because they did not receive the love of the truth so as to be saved.

For this reason God will send upon them a deluding influence so that they will believe what is false, in order that they all may be judged who did not believe the truth, but took pleasure in wickedness.

2 Thess. 2:1–12 (NASB)

The word "apostasy" used here in the NASB, was interpreted as "a falling away," in the King James Version and probably other versions of the Bible as well. This new rendering is more exact and means a renunciation of a major religion, and Paul was speaking about an apostasy or a renunciation of the Christian faith. The Greek word used in the original writing can be translated both as a renunciation and a falling away; however, a falling away would be an apostasy from within the order, while a renouncement must come from without. When you study what Paul has said, it is apparent that the apostasy is from a source outside the Christian faith. The Koran is a complete renunciation of Christianity, therefore; the apostasy has occurred already. There is no need to expect a falling away from the Christian faith from within.

ISLAM, THE APOSTASY OF CHRISTIANITY

The "apostasy," requires a renunciation of Christianity by a major force, and must also involve theology. Since this apostasy will be observable by all Christians, it must be widespread and recognizable. The Jews denied the divinity of Christ because he came without being like they expected, and this difference of opinion existed as Paul was writing, so they cannot be considered the apostasy.

The only situation that fulfills Paul's apostasy is the rise of Islam and the Muslim inquisition. The opposing theology is involved and the whole of Christianity was aware of the competing force; and they reacted with military action, the Crusades, against the intruding power. The Crusades were unsuccessful because of logistics; however, the advance of Islam was slowed.

Islam is the only world power that promotes a theology that is diametrically opposed to Christianity, and Paul refers to this theology as lawlessness because it professes rules to live by that are opposite what Jesus taught and what God has published in the Bible and referred to as "the Law." People who know what the Bible teaches can readily recognize the opposing theology of the Koran by reading the summary of the Koran included in this treatise.

In the Koran, at Sura (chapter) III, verses 1 and 2, the god of the Koran claims to be the only God and claims to have "sent down the Law and the Evangel (previous scripture) aforetime, as man's guidance." Thus, the Muslims are taught that their god is the same deity that was worshipped by Abraham, Moses, the Jews, and the Christians. Nothing could be farther from the truth. This teaching from the Koran also fulfills Paul's prophesy that; "the man of lawlessness, the son of destruction, who opposes and exalts himself above every so-called god or object of worship," will be revealed.

When I look at the obvious anti-Christian teachings in the Koran, I am surprised that the Christian community has not spoken out loudly that the god of the Koran is not the same god as our God. A concerted effort to publicize this fact would serve to greatly ameliorate the threat of Muslim dominance throughout the world. There has been a lack of study within the Christian community on the teachings of Islam. We have relinquished our position as the world's most important religion for naught and remained silent while Satan scores many points throughout the world.

Regardless of what the world calls Islam or what it names itself; it is a cult, the world's largest cult. Look at the design of it and see that it meets every requirement in mind control of its followers, and in the social mores necessary for membership. Membership is not optional and a member cannot leave the fold and live.

The mind control exerted upon the Muslims makes Paul's description of a deluding influence understandable. The Koran describes a Christian as "one who joins gods with God." Mohammad coined this descriptive phrase because of the Christian belief in the deity of Christ and the Holy Spirit. The God to whom we join Christ and the Holy Spirit is the God of the Bible. The teachings of the Koran prove that the god of the

PORK, BEEF, CHICKEN AND RIBS

Bible is not the god of the Koran, because the teachings are very different and conflict with each other.

It seems to be completely unrealistic that laws and mores existing throughout the world since the beginning of time could be so upended in so short a time as one generation, but Islam did just that throughout Arabia, during Mohammad's lifetime. Laws were radically changed, human values negated, common sense rules of property ownership skewed to place women in disfavor, and the truth condemned to the trash heap.

What is the reasoning behind these changes? Number one is the physical superiority of men over women and the seductive sex drive, characteristic of Baal worship. It is barbaric to consider women inferior to man, but this religion does that by relegating their position to a chattel. The religion of Islam promotes the monopolistic avarice and greed for position and power. Islam did not want to only be the main or leading religion in the minds of mankind, but the only religion. The Koran tells some of the complaints received from those people being coerced during the process of eliminating other religions, such as that coercion during the sacred months when the people must make the choice to join, or to leave, or to stay and die. When I read these complaints, I can feel the anguish of those people who must make their choice. The writing also demonstrates the consternation of Mohammad when he knows that many of the people don't believe but joined just to survive. You must hold your mouth just right, put your hands in the proper posture, and bow down just so; every move is scripted to control the mind of the individual and take choice away. You must not expect to make a choice. You must conform to the demands of the author of the play or not be a part of the cast.

When Muslims become the dominant power in an area, they must purge that area of non-believers (infidels). The Muslims establish a period of four months in which any infidel may convert to Islam, make a treaty with Islam under which a fee is levied, or leave that area. They call this four months time period, "the sacred months;" and the infidels can go at large (unencumbered or free) in the land during that four month period. Here are the instructions to the "believers" after these four months.

> And when the sacred months are past, kill those who join other gods with God wherever ye shall find them; and seize them, besiege them, and lay wait for them with every kind of ambush; but if they shall convert, and observe prayer, and pay the obligatory alms, then let them go their way, for God is gracious, merciful.
>
> Sura 9:5 (Koran)

During the Muslim inquisition when Yemen was converted, the Jews there made a treaty with the Caliph and lived in peace with the Muslims until the nation of Israel was reformed by the United Nations after World War II. Now contrast this teaching with what Jesus taught (Matt. 5:44): "But I say to you, love your enemies and do good to those who hate you."

Surely the Christians of the free world can do something to bring about the enlightenment in the lives of our Muslim neighbors; for there are a multitude of fathers who find themselves on the precipice similar to Mahmod Mahmod who was found guilty of murder after killing his daughter in an "honor" killing. Logic should tell the Muslims that the proofs of the accuracy of the Christian Bible are irrefutable. The proofs are substantial and convincing to the rest of the world, so why do they continue to proclaim the Bible as false. Logic tells me that a God who insists that he does not change, will not profess one thing for three thousand years, and then reverse his position expressly for a part of the world. Logic also tells me that the teachings of the true God will withstand scrutiny from any source.

To the pure, all things are pure; but to those who are defiled and unbelieving, nothing is pure, but both their mind and their conscience are defiled. They profess to know God, but by their deeds they deny him, being detestable and disobedient and worthless for any good deed.

Titus 1:15–16 (NASB)

If anyone advocates a different doctrine and does not agree with sound words, those of our Lord Jesus Christ, and with the doctrine conforming to godliness, he is conceited and understands nothing; but he has a morbid interest in controversial questions and disputes about words, out of which arise envy, strife, abusive language, evil suspicions, and constant friction between men of depraved mind and deprived of the truth, who supposes that godliness is a means of gain.

1 Timothy 6:3–5 (NASB)

Look now at the practices within the Muslim faith that identifies it as a cult. The Koran prohibits the Muslim from making friends with Christians or anyone outside Islam, so the believer is insulated from any other religious influence. There are 250 passages within the Koran that the devout believer must memorize and must also recognize the passages that lead into those passages that are identified by the word "Say", so that they are able to orally say those passages when the leader from the podium reads the passage and reaches the word "Say." The Islamic religious school where the young boys are trained in the faith is called a "madrassa" and usually the twelve-year-old males are sent there. This is where they memorize the necessary parts of the Koran and all the necessary body movements and positions to conform to accepted practice.

It is forbidden for a member of the Muslim religion to leave the religion. There was a report from London of an "honor" killing where a fifty-two-year-old father, Mahmod Mahmod, held a family meeting where it was decided that his twenty-year-old daughter Banaz, must die because she fell in love with a non-Muslim man; most likely a Christian. She was strangled with a bootlace, stuffed into a suitcase, and buried in the back garden. Her death was only one in an increasing number of such killings in Britain, home to some 1.8 million Muslims. The news article from London states that there are more than 100 homicides under investigation as potential "honor" killings. Logic and Common sense is missing in these situations.

Islam is the largest religious cult in the world and logic is not a part of the thoughts of their believers. In order for such obvious crimes to be perpetrated upon the people, there must be a religious leader involved that adheres to the strict rules of Islam for his followers; and then his followers must believe that the leader is infallible and relegate their own natural feelings, and accept these absolute and unnatural teachings to be proper. The strict rules imposed upon the Muslim people control their lives in every way—Control that free people, not brought up under these strict rules, would never accept and find hard even to understand.

The Koran forbids the believer from taking as friends, people of other religions; thus, the social environment for the Muslim is controlled by Islamic law and the people must conform to that law or be ostracized by the community. The Koran establishes times for the people to pray, and these times are usually stated as daybreak, mid-day, and nighttime. When we read this in the Koran, it does not sound unreasonable, and there is no reaction from non-believers until the call to prayer is heard from the mosque before daybreak, designed to wake the people so that the devout may attend the morning prayer. There is at least one slender lofty tower called a minaret, attached to the mosque with a balcony from which the muezzin, or Muslim crier summons the people to prayer; however, today, electronic speakers are used. Every day for the Muslim, starts with a reinforcement of the mind control that the religion maintains over its people. This control is reinforced again at noon and again in the evening; and this is every day of the week—every week.

BRAINWASHING

There is no freedom for those who practice Islam. Perhaps this is what Christ recognized when he said: "If you continue in my word then you are truly disciples of mine, and you will know the truth, and the truth will make you free" (John 8:31–32 NASB). The people who conform to the teachings of the Koran are certainly not free. The mind control that Islam develops over the individual is astonishing. The believer has received so much indoctrination that they have lost the ability to think logically in matters that do not agree with the Koran. They have been deceived, and they have been brainwashed. Compare how the definition of "brainwashing" or coercive persuasion coincides with Islam.

> A systematic effort to persuade nonbelievers to accept a certain allegiance, command or doctrine. A colloquial term, it is more generally applied to any technique designed to manipulate human thought or action against the desire, will, or knowledge of the individual. By controlling the physical and social environment, an attempt is made to destroy loyalties to an individual's former loyalties and beliefs, and to substitute loyalty to a new ideology or power. It has been used by religious cults as well as by radical political groups. The techniques of brainwashing usually involve isolation from former associates and

sources of information; and exacting regimen calling for absolute obedience, and humility; strong social pressures, and rewards for cooperation; physical and psychological punishments for noncooperation, including social ostracism and criticism, deprivation of food, sleep, and social contacts, bondage, and torture; and constant reinforcement. Its effects are sometimes reversed through deprogramming which combines confrontation and intensive psychotherapy.

Brainwashing from Wikipedia

A very good description brainwashing is available from the Encyclopedia Britannica, also called Coercive Persuasion. That article is not included here because of copyright issues and the length of the article. It is available from the Internet.

The young sons of Islam follow their fathers to the mosque where strict regimen is employed to cause the religion to become the foremost experience in their lives. Only the men and boys are permitted in the main gathering hall where the ritual prayers (Salat) are performed. The men gather in precise rows, properly spaced, and do exact body movements (Rakat) in preparation for prayer. The kneeling position with the forehead touching the floor is the picture usually seen of the congregation in Muslim prayer. This position requires that the palms of the hands, the knees, and the toes of both feet also touch the floor. A position called bowing follows the kneeling posture and the back should be straight so that a glass of water placed on the back will not spill. Even the fingers and toes are positioned for conformity. It is required that the first chapter (Sura 1) of the Koran be memorized and said in unison at the start of salat, and this is a short praise to the God of the Koran. During the rakat, other phrases are also repeated which include twice denying Christianity, with phrases denoting that there are no partners with God. The rakats must be accomplished facing toward the Ka'ba in Mecca, and are completed in a kneeling posture. The leader will read from the Koran and the congregation must respond in unison to passages that have a response written into the Koran; therefore, it is necessary that they memorize much of the Koran. There are over 250 such written passages, preceded by *Say* or *And Say* which call for a response from the listener.

We have concerned ourselves with what we need to do to prepare ourselves for the coming of Christ and have overlooked what is happening to those people holding to a false belief that has been championed by demons, in that part of the world ransomed to Satan. Simply put, the wrath of God is resting on their shoulders, and their blind attempts to reach a deity who has deceived them into thinking he is god, is wreaking havoc in their lives. Banaz Mahmod is just one of many young people who are offsprings of Muslim believers caught up in a more enlightened world; a world that is recognizing Islam in its true attire.

Read again what John the Baptist said about these lost souls: "The Father loves the Son and has given all things into his hand. He who believes in the Son has eternal life; but he who does not obey the Son will not see life, but the wrath of God abides on him," (John 3:36, NASB).

Banaz Mahmod was attempting to move away from that darkness. Light has come into the world, and men loved the darkness rather than the light, for their deeds were evil.

Moses said, "The Lord God will raise up for you a prophet like me from your brethren; to him you shall give heed to everything he says to you. And it will be that every soul that does not heed that prophet shall be utterly destroyed from among the people" (Acts 3:22 –23, NASB). Mahmod Mahmod is utterly destroyed as a father. And Paul said, "God, after he spoke long ago to the fathers in the prophets in many portions and in many ways, in these last days has spoken to us in his Son, whom he appointed heir of all things, through whom also he made the world. And he is the radiance of his glory and the exact representation of his nature and upholds all things by the word of his power (Hebrews 1:1–2 NASB). Mahmod Mahmod's ears were closed to what was spoken by the Son of God.

I read in Time magazine what Mariane Pearl said to a questioner about how her view of Islam might have changed after Muslims murdered her husband, and her reply was, "No, it hasn't changed at all. I grew up with Muslim people, so I was very acquainted with Islam. So it is not like the people who killed Danny taught me what Islam was about. They are hijackers of their own faith." She was familiar with Muslims that had no reason to oppose her, but not with the teachings of the Koran. Other people speak of the moderate Muslim as though they do not subscribe to the same Koran that the Wahhabi sect, who murdered Danny Pearl, and other militant Muslims, subscribe to. I have studied the Koran and read it through about ten times, and studied parts of it in detail and the teachings are there to kill the infidels, and to lay ambush for them, and cut off their heads and every finger also. It is written in the Koran for anyone to read, and the book gives the believer no discretion in the policy. The al-Qaeda does not have a Koran that is different. The militant Muslim is not exaggerating or teaching anything that is not written, many times, in the Koran; and they call upon the son of destruction as god.

A news article about Turkey by Marc Champion, published December 17, 2010, quoted Turkey's Army Gen. Cetin Dugan, who makes no effort to disguise his hostility to the Islamic-leaning Justice and Development Party, or AKP, many of whose leaders were part of the regime he helped drive from power thirteen years earlier. "Once they (the AKP) have power all to themselves they will make Turkey like Iran, step by step, I see it heading that way," said General Dogan.

He said westerners who believe "mild Muslims" can lead Turkey to democracy were naive, because avowed Muslims will always refer to the Quran, no matter how moderate. Recent happenings in Turkey seem to substantiate General Dogan"s forecast of actions by the ruling AKP party as they take the country backwards into the Sharia-dominated lifestyle.

THE CONFLICTING THEOLOGIES

The theologies taught in the Koran are usually opposite or conflicting with the teachings of Christianity. One of the most noticeable is the requirement that the believer takes vengeance for his god against their enemies or the infidels. The God of the Bible teaches that he is the one to take vengeance, and prohibits the faithful from doing harm to anyone. The true God taught (Deut. 32:35, Rom. 12:19), "Vengeance is mine, I will repay", and tells adherents to love their enemies, to feed them if they are hungry, and give them water to drink if they thirst.

Then the true God guarantees that the transgressor will fall in due time, meaning when he decides to take vengeance. The true God prohibited Satan from taking the life of Job when he gave Job into Satan's hand (Job 1:12). This scripture teaches that Satan does not have the power to take a human life: so, therefore, written into the Muslim holy book is the requirement for the Muslim believer to take vengeance against his corporate enemies. Note that in the following passage it is claimed that he (the God of the Koran) could, if he wished, take vengeance himself. This is a false claim.

When ye encounter the infidels, strike off their heads till ye have made a great slaughter among them, and of the rest make fast the fetters. And afterwards let there either be free dismissals or ransomings till the war hath laid down its burdens. Thus do. Were such the pleasure of God, he could himself take vengeance upon them: but he would rather prove the one of you by the other. And who so fight for the cause of God, their words he will not suffer to miscarry; he will vouchsafe them guidance, and dispose their hearts aright; and he will bring them into the Paradise, of which he hath told them. Believers! If ye help God, God will help you, and will set your feet firm: But as for the infidels, let them perish: and their works shall God bring to naught: This—because God is the protector of those who believe, and because the infidels have no protector.

Sura 47:4–12 (Koran)

A *beheading* is indicative of a religious killing by a Muslim, because it is the prescribed method taught in the Koran. At Sura 8:12 it is taught to strike off their heads and every fingertip also. At 5:37, it is taught to slay or crucify or cut off alternate hands and feet. There are about fourteen other verses in the Koran that direct the Muslim to slay the infidels, and the Koran does not mention a method to employ them. I know of no other society that will accept mutilation of a corpse, much less condone the practice. Remember when you read from the Koran that an infidel is a Christian, and God is the god of the Koran. There is also a passage at Sura 17:61 to explain why no miracles are being performed, with this statement: "Nothing hindered us from sending thee with the power of working miracles, except that the people of old treated them as lies."

Another grave error made by the Muslim believer is to consider a woman as less important than a man and look upon the woman as a possession of a man. The God of the Bible considers man and woman to be equal, and designed to complement each other. The Bible teaches that marriage is joining one man and one woman together. The true God states that a man and a woman when joined in holy matrimony, become one. Hebrews 13:4 states: "Marriage is to be held in honor among all, and the marriage bed is to be undefiled (do not corrupt the purity or perfection of the sexual relationship between husband and wife); for fornicators and adulterers God will judge." God loved Jacob but hated his twin brother Esau. Esau became a polygamist which is a practice hated by the true God. Paul, in his writing to Timothy reiterates the warning of the apostasy and his description accurately fits the Islamist.

> But the Spirit explicitly says that in the later times some will fall away from the faith, paying attention to deceitful spirits and doctrines of demons, by means of the hypocrisy of liars seared in their own conscience as with a branding iron, men who forbid marriage and advocate abstaining from foods which God has created to be gratefully shared in by those who believe and know the truth. For everything created by God is good, and nothing is to be rejected if it is received with gratitude.
>
> 1 Tim. 4:1–4, (NASB)

The Greek word, "koluo" was translated here as, "forbid." A better translation for, "koluo," would be "interfere with," for the primary meaning of the word is "to hinder." Islam does not forbid marriage, but by promoting polygamy, it does hinder marriage. Islam does forbid the eating of pork and drinking of alcoholic beverages. I am impressed by the way Paul's words, "seared in their own conscience as with a branding iron," because that description fits the cult mindset of the Muslim.

The true God does not respect the rich more than he does the poor, nor the strong more than he does the weak, nor the man more than he does the woman. This teaching stems from God giving the law to Moses and was first given in the context of judges making decisions in matters before them. Justice is to be administered to all people in a like manner, and their worldly possessions or their worldly position should not be a factor in determining guilt or innocence. This impartiality of God extends to all human relations, even to the seating of congregants in the temple. According to the teachings of the Koran, men are more important than women and the rich are considered more important than the poor. This is wrong in the eyes of the true God.

Another error perpetrated by the author of the Koran is the practice of Takiyya, or deception (pronounced tark-e-ya). The teaching is that if a person will be endangered or belittled in revealing his or her true belief in Islam, then they may deny his or her Muslim belief with permission from his or her their god, if his or her heart remains committed to Islam. This is lying with approval from their God. The true God does not approve of a lie in any form, and makes the truth a major requirement for the Christian believer. One of the Ten Commandments states that you must not bear false witness. A false witness will pervert justice, and the true God promotes justice for all people without partiality. One of the last warnings in the Bible is Rev. 22:15 which condemns all liars. Christians must not fail to acknowledge Jesus Christ as Lord. The teachings of Jesus in his words is this: "Whoever denies me before men, I will also deny him before my Father in Heaven." In Josh. 24:27, denying the God of the Bible was prohibited. The marked difference in these teachings requires that the inspiration behind them come from different deities.

The mutilation of a human body is despicable to all people, including the followers of Islam. The ungodly and inhuman treatment of women is being rejected all over the world, and Muslim nations are not immune from the hatred of women who disagree with that Islamic teaching. In national politics, the lies emanating from the practice of Takiyya (deception) have resulted in a situation where no one believes anything proposed by Islamist; and after years of Yasser Arafat with his deceptive practices, the world is justified in this attitude. It is time now for all people of the world to reject these ungodly teachings. From the teachings of Paul, we now know that the god of the Koran is the antichrist of the Bible; therefore, we have two inspired books emanating from the spiritual world: the Bible coming from God the Almighty, the Creator, the God of Heaven, and the Koran coming from Satan, God of the world, the antichrist.

THE GATHERING OF GOD'S PEOPLE

As mankind evolved and when the time was right, God selected one man, Abraham, to be the man through which he would bring salvation to the world. God made a covenant with Abraham and said to him; "Go forth from your country, and from your relatives and from your fathers house, to the land which I will show you; and I will make you a great nation, and I will bless you, and make your name great; and so you shall be a blessing; and I will bless those who bless you, and the one who curses you I will curse. And in you all the families of the earth will be blessed."

Abraham followed God and so became a great man for that time, and he had a son Isaac who also followed God and came to know him. Isaac became the father of Jacob who in like manner came to know God and to follow him. God changed Jacob's name to Israel and made the same covenant with Israel that had been made with his father and grandfather. Israel had twelve sons who became the patriarchs of the twelve tribes referred to by the name, "Hebrew" because they originated from Hebron in the land of Canaan. They and their descendants are also called the children of Israel. Of the twelve, Joseph was Israel's favorite and became the heir of the covenant, and was favored by God.

What is important to remember is God's promise that through Abraham, all the families of the earth will be blessed.

Joseph's older brothers hated him because he was favored above them and finding an opportunity to dispose of him, sold him as a slave to some traders en route to Egypt. Joseph was sold as a slave to Potiphar, the captain of the bodyguard for Pharaoh. The Lord was with Joseph and he prospered in Egypt, and became known for his ability to interpret dreams through God, whom he served. Joseph interpreted Pharaoh's dream of a coming seven years of plenty, followed by seven years of famine; and so impressed Pharaoh that he became the highest official in the land, and supervised the storage of grain during the good years and disbursement of it during the lean years, and he became famous in all of Egypt. The famine caused the children of Israel to seek relief from Egypt and they were reunited with Joseph; and in due course, came to live in Egypt. The Hebrew people who came to Egypt from Canaan numbered only about seventy-seven, and they prospered, and they multiplied in the land.

Throughout the years Joseph died and a new Pharaoh came to power that did not know him. Over time the Hebrews became slaves in Egypt. The Hebrews multiplied faster than did the Egyptians, and the Pharaoh became fearful that they would become great enough to overpower his people, so he declared that all male children born to the Hebrews were to be cast into the Nile. Now, a man from the branch of Levi went and married a daughter of Levi. The woman conceived and bore a son who was so beautiful that she hid him for three months. When she could hide him no longer, she got a wicker basket and covered it over with tar and pitch so that it would float, and set it in the reeds along the bank of the Nile. His sister stood at a distance to find out what would happen to him. The daughter of Pharaoh came down to bathe, with her maidens walking alongside the Nile; and she saw the basket among the reeds and sent her maid, and she brought it to her. When she saw the baby she had pity on him. Then the sister of Moses who had been watching him

PORK, BEEF, CHICKEN AND RIBS

said to Pharaoh's daughter, "Shall I go and call a nurse for you from the Hebrew women that she might nurse the child for you?" Pharaoh's daughter said, "go ahead." So the girl went and told their mother. Then Pharaoh's daughter said to her, "Take this child away and nurse him for me, and I will give you your wages." So the woman took the child and nursed him, and the child grew, and she brought him to Pharaoh's daughter and he became her adopted son, and she named him Moses.

Moses grew up in the household of the Pharaoh but with the knowledge that he was a Hebrew. When he was forty years old he saw an Egyptian mistreating a Hebrew man and was angry, and slew the Egyptian. When Pharaoh heard of this he attempted to find Moses to kill him, but Moses escaped to the wilderness of Haran. There he made his life shepherding sheep; married and had two sons with his wife Zipporah. While he was keeping the sheep of Jetro, his father-in-law, he saw a bush on fire, but the bush was not being consumed; and as he approached the bush, God spoke to him. God made Moses the agent through whom he would free the Hebrew children from the bondage of the Egyptians. We know that God planned some notoriety for that act by what he told Moses to say before Pharaoh. God was unknown outside the Hebrew descendants of Abraham.

> Then the Lord said to Moses, "Rise up early in the morning and stand before Pharaoh and say to him, 'Thus says the Lord, the God of the Hebrews, "Let my people go, that they may serve me. For this time I will send all my plagues on you and your servants and your people, so that you may know that there is no one like me in all the earth. For if by now I had put forth my hand and struck you and your people with pestilence, you would then have been cut off from the earth. But, indeed, for this reason I have allowed you to remain, in order to show you my power and in order to proclaim my name through all the earth.
>
> Exodus 9:13–16 (NASB)

So we know that God expected to gain a reputation "through all the earth" for the demonstration of his power before Pharaoh which resulted in the Exodus. We know from reading of Balak, king of Moab and Balaam the diviner in Numbers 22–24 that God's reputation was well known during the time of the Exodus. God told of the gathering together of his people Israel through Nathan the Prophet when David wanted to build him a house.

> Go and say to my servant David, 'Thus says the Lord, "Are you the one who should build me a house to dwell in? For I have not dwelt in a house since the day I brought up the sons of Israel from Egypt, even to this day; but I have been moving about in a tent, even in a tabernacle. Wherever I have gone with all the sons of Israel, did I speak a word with one of the tribes of Israel, which I commanded to shepherd my people Israel, saying, 'Why have you not built me a house of cedar? Now therefore, thus you shall say to my servant David, 'Thus says the Lord of hosts, "I took you from the pasture, from following the sheep, to be ruler over my people Israel.
>
> I have been with you wherever you have gone and have cut off all your enemies from before you; and I will make you a great name, like the names of the great men who are on the earth. I will also appoint a place for my people Israel and will plant them, that they may live in their own place and not be disturbed again, nor will the wicked afflict them any more as formerly, even from the day that I commanded judges to be over my people Israel; and I will give you rest from all your enemies.
>
> The Lord also declares to you that the Lord will make a house for you. When your days are complete and you lie down with your fathers, I will raise up your descendant after you, who will come forth from you, and I will establish his kingdom. He shall build a house for my name, and I will establish the throne of his kingdom forever. I will be a father to him and he will be a son to me; when he commits

iniquity, I will correct him with the rod of men and the strokes of the sons of men, but my lovingkindness shall not depart from him, as I took it away from Saul, whom I removed from before you.

Your house and your kingdom shall endure before me forever; your throne shall be established forever. In accordance with all these words and all this vision, so Nathan spoke to David.

2 Samuel 7:5–17 (NASB)

Now God tells that he will be known more for gathering his people together than he was for bringing them out of Egypt. It is forecast two times in Jeremiah that God will become known for his gathering together the *children* of God from the north land and from all the countries where he had driven them so that they would live securely on their own soil.

> Behold, the days are coming, declares the Lord, "when I will raise up for David a righteous branch; and he will reign as king and act wisely and do justice and righteousness in the land; in his days Judah will be saved and Israel will dwell securely; and this is his name by which he will be called, 'the Lord our righteousness.'" "Therefore behold, the days are coming," declares the Lord, "when they will no longer say, 'as the Lord lives, who brought up the sons of Israel from the land of Egypt,' but 'as the Lord lives, who brought up and led back the descendants of the household of Israel from the North land and from all the countries where I had driven them. Then they will live on their own soil."

Jeremiah 23:5–8 (NASB)

Therefore behold, days are coming," declares the Lord, "when it will no longer be said, 'As the Lord lives, who brought up the sons of Israel out of the land of Egypt,' but, 'As the Lord lives, who brought up the sons of Israel from the land of the north and from all the countries where he had banished them.' For I will restore them to their own land which I gave to their fathers.

Jeremiah 16:14–15 (NASB)

This prophesy recalls the notoriety of God which resulted from him bringing the Hebrew children out of Egypt following the tenth and final plague on Pharaoh's people, the miracle of the Passover, and states that days are coming when he will be remembered more for the gathering together of his children from all parts of the earth, to have them dwell safely in their own land. God has already accomplished this great thing. He has gathered together his people from all parts of the earth for them to dwell in their own land in safety and freedom, where justice prevails.

This gathering together is for the new Israel of God, who are his children by way of the new covenant and named Christians because of their faith in Jesus Christ. This gathering was accomplished when people from all over Europe immigrated to America. Freedom to worship as they pleased was the main reason for the mass movement of people and this is what God wants to be known for; the gathering together of the Christian people to America. Following God's announcement of the ransom, He tells of this gathering.

> Do not fear, for I am with you; I will bring your offspring from the east, And gather you from the west. "I will say to the north, 'Give them up!' And to the south, 'Do not hold them back.' Bring my sons from afar and my daughters from the ends of the earth, everyone who is called by my name, and whom I have created for my glory, whom I have formed, even whom I have made.
>
> Isaiah 43:5–7 (NASB)

PORK, BEEF, CHICKEN AND RIBS

When America was being populated, one of the main reasons for the mass immigration was people seeking religious freedom, and this remains a major reason for people to come to America even today. A gathering together would be unlikely today because every square foot of the world geography is known, and is controlled by a government entity. The upbeat description in Isaiah about the new land which his people will be gathered too has the characteristics of the United States of today. Compare this country as you know it to the description of the new Zion.

> Arise, shine; for your light has come, and the glory of the Lord has risen upon you. For behold, darkness will cover the earth and deep darkness the peoples; but the Lord will rise upon you and his glory will appear upon you. Nations will come to your light, and kings to the brightness of your rising. Lift up your eyes round about and see; they all gather together, they come to you. Your sons will come from afar, and your daughters will be carried in the arms.
>
> Then you will see and be radiant, and your heart will thrill and rejoice; because the abundance of the sea will be turned to you, the wealth of the nations will come to you. A multitude of camels will cover you, the young camels of Midian and Ephah; all those from Sheba will come; they will bring gold and frankincense, and will bear good news of the praises of the Lord.
>
> All the flocks of Kedar will be gathered together to you, the rams of Nebaioth will minister to you; they will go up with acceptance on My altar, and I shall glorify my glorious house. Who are these who fly like a cloud and like the doves to their lattices? Surely the coastlands will wait for me; and the ships of Tarshish will come first, to bring your sons from afar; their silver and their gold with them, for the name of the Lord your God, and for the Holy One of Israel because he has glorified you.
>
> Foreigners will buildup your walls and their kings will minister to you; for in my wrath I struck you, and in

my favor I have had compassion on you. Your gates will be open continually; they will not be closed day or night, so that men may bring to you the wealth of the nations, with their kings led in procession. For the nation and the kingdom which will not serve you will perish and the nations will be utterly ruined.

The glory of Lebanon will come to you, the juniper, the box tree and the cypress together. To beautify the place of my sanctuary; and I shall make the place of my feet glorious. The sons of those who afflicted you will come bowing to you, and all those who despised you will bow themselves at the soles of your feet; and they will call you the city of the Lord, the Zion of the Holy One of Israel.

Whereas you have been forsaken and hated with no one passing through, I will make you an everlasting pride, a joy from generation to generation. You will also suck the milk of nations and suck the breast of kings; then you will know that I the Lord, am your Savior and your redeemer, the Mighty One of Jacob.

Isaiah 60:1–16 (NASB)

The Christian people of the world are the "Israel of God"; and while that name applies to all of God's children, the greatest concentration is here, in the United States of America. Justice is more abundant here than any other nation on earth, and that is God's favorite element in a government. Justice is joy to the righteous but terror to the workers of iniquity (Prov. 21:15 NASB). The defining passage that convinced me that the US is the new Zion comes in Is. 60:5, where it is stated: "the wealth of the nations will come to you." That is certainly true today in this country because we consume a much greater portion of the world's production than any other population. The Christian Churches of Ireland were catalyst for groups coming to this new land, when the gathering together of the Christian people to America was under way. There were many instigators of the influx

PORK, BEEF, CHICKEN AND RIBS

of people to America in addition to the religious motivation. The potato famine, the exorbitant rents imposed on the farmers of Ireland by the English landlords, and the desire to own the land. My forefathers in a Presbyterian congregation in Ireland, decided to join with another congregation in order to hire a ship to take them to America. By the time of sailing, there were five congregations and three ships commissioned to make the trip, and they arrived at Charleston harbor in the fall of 1752. When Colonial Plats were laid out, one hundred acres was allowed for the head of household and fifty cress for each other member of the family. My forefather receiving the land was given three hundred acres along the Broad river for himself, his wife, and three children. Good things continue to be prophesied for the new Israel by Isaiah that continued to include characteristics of the USA.

> Then they will rebuild the ancient ruins, they will raise up the former devastations; and they will repair the ruined cities, the desolations of many generations. Strangers will stand and pasture your flocks, and foreigners will be your farmers and your vinedressers. But you will be called the priests of the Lord; you will be spoken of as ministers of our God. You will eat the wealth of nations and in their riches you will boast. Instead of your shame you will have a double portion, and instead of humiliation they will shout for joy over their portion. Therefore, they will possess a double portion in their land, everlasting joy will be theirs for I, the Lord, love justice, I hate robbery in the burnt offering; and I will faithfully give them their recompense and make an everlasting covenant with them. Then their offspring will be known among the nations, and their descendants in the midst of the peoples. All who see them will recognize them because they are the offspring whom the Lord has blessed.
>
> Isaiah 61:4–9 (NASB)

Here the statement, "Strangers will stand and pasture your flocks, and foreigners will be your farmers and vinedressers," is descriptive of the America today. Ezekiel gives a vision of the gathering together of God's people that includes the identifying phrase of new covenant people; "Then they will be my people, and I shall be their God."

> Therefore say, "Thus, says the Lord God, 'I will gather you from the peoples and assemble you out of the countries among which you have been scattered, and I will give you the land of Israel.' When they come there, they will remove all its detestable things and all its abominations from it. And I will give them one heart, and put a new spirit within them. And I will take the heart of stone out of their flesh and give them a heart of flesh, that they may walk in my statures and keep my ordinances and do them. Then they will be my people, and I shall be their God. But as for those whose hearts go after their detestable things and abominations, I will bring their conduct down on their heads," declares the Lord God.
>
> Ezekiel 11:17–21 (NASB)

This gathering together from Ezekiel chapter 11 could be a symbolic gathering into a universal church of like-minded people, but it could also be applied to the geographical gathering of his people to this free land. While a symbolic gathering could be intended here, a geographical gathering is necessary for God to gain the notoriety of "placing them on their own soil," that he proclaims in Jeremiah 23:8; for that notoriety must be recognized throughout the whole world, as it was in the seventeenth and eighteenth centuries.

Ezekiel foretells the gathering together again in chapter 34 and here the reason for God's forming a new Israel is explained and a more definitive description of the gathering together to

PORK, BEEF, CHICKEN AND RIBS

this land is given; even to calling the new land a "renowned planting place." The shepherds here are the religious leaders who have excluded from the temple the sick, the infirm, the deformed, the unclean, and many other people who did not measure up to the standards set by them for temple access. It was this omission of many people from their religious activities that caused Jesus to accuse the Pharisees of teaching as doctrine the precepts of men.

> And he said to them, "Rightly did Isaiah prophesy of you hypocrites, as it is written: 'these people honor me with their lips, but their heart is far away from me. But in vain do they worship me, teaching as doctrines the precepts of men. Neglecting the commandment of God, you hold to the tradition of men.
>
> Mark 7:6–9 (NASB)

He was also saying to them, "You are experts at setting aside the commandment of God in order to keep your tradition."

> Then the word of the Lord came to me saying, "Son of man, prophesy against the shepherds of Israel. Prophesy and say to those shepherds, 'Thus says the Lord God,'" "Woe, shepherds of Israel who have been feeding themselves! Should not the shepherds feed the flock?" "You eat the fat and clothe yourselves with the wool; you slaughter the fat sheep without feeding the flock." Those who are sickly you have not strengthened, the diseased you have not healed, the broken you have not bound up, the scattered you have not brought back, nor have you sought for the lost; but with force and with severity you have dominated them." They were scattered for lack of a shepherd, and they became food for every beast of the field and were scattered.
>
> "My flock wandered through all the mountains and on every high hill; my flock was scattered over all the surface of the earth, and there was no one to search or seek for them. Therefore, you shepherds, hear the word of the

Lord: "As I live," declares the Lord God, "surely because my flock has become a prey, my flock has even become food for all the beasts of the field for lack of a shepherd, and my shepherds did not search for my flock, but rather the shepherds fed themselves and did not feed my flock; therefore, you shepherds, hear the word of the Lord: 'thus says the Lord God, "Behold, I am against the shepherds, and I will demand my sheep from them and make them cease from feeding sheep. So the shepherds will not feed themselves anymore, but I will deliver my flock from their mouth, so that they will not be food for them."

For thus says the Lord God, "Behold, I myself will search for my sheep and seek them out. "As a shepherd cares for his herd in the day when he is among his scattered sheep, so I will care for my sheep and will deliver them from all the places to which they were scattered on a cloudy and gloomy day. "I will bring them out from the peoples and gather them from the countries and bring them to their own land; and I will feed them on the mountains of Israel, by the streams, and in all the inhabited places of the land.

"I will feed them in a good pasture, and their grazing ground will be on the mountain heights of Israel. There they will lie down on good grazing ground and feed in rich pasture on the mountains of Israel. "I will feed my flock and I will lead them to rest," declares the Lord God.

"I will seek the lost, bring back the scattered, bind up the broken and strengthen the sick; but the fat and the strong I will destroy. I will feed them with judgment. "As for you, my flock, thus says the Lord God, 'Behold, I will judge between one sheep and another, between the rams and the male goats.

'Is it too slight a thing for you that you should feed in the good pasture that you must tread down with your feet the rest of your pastures? Or that you should drink of the clear waters, that you must foul the rest with your feet? 'As

PORK, BEEF, CHICKEN AND RIBS

for my flock, they must eat what you tread down with your feet and drink what you foul with your feet!'

"Therefore, thus says the Lord God to them, "Behold, I, even I, will judge between the fat sheep and the lean sheep. "Because you push with side and with shoulder, and thrust at all the weak with your horns until you have scattered them abroad, therefore, I will deliver my flock, and they will no longer be a prey; and I will judge between one sheep and another.

"Then I will set over them one shepherd, my servant David, and he will feed them; he will feed them himself and be their shepherd. "And I, the Lord, will be their God, and my servant David will be prince among them; I the Lord have spoken. "I will make a covenant of peace with them and eliminate harmful beasts from the land so that they may live securely in the wilderness and sleep in the woods.

"I will make them and the places around My hill a blessing. And I will cause showers to come down in their season; they will be showers of blessing. "Also the tree of the field will yield its fruit and the earth will yield its increase, and they will be secure on their land. Then they will know that I am the Lord, when I have broken the bars of their yoke and have delivered them from the hand of those who enslaved them.

"They will no longer be a prey to the nations, and the beasts of the earth will not devour them; but they will live securely, and no one will make them afraid. "I will establish for them a renowned planting place, and they will not again be victims of famine in the land, and they will not endure the insults of the nations anymore. "Then they will know that I, the Lord their God, am with them, and that they, the house of Israel, are my people," declares the Lord God. "As for you, my sheep, the sheep of my pasture, you are men, and I am your God," declares the Lord God.

Ezekiel 34:1–31 (NASB)

The shepherds here are the religious leaders who have excluded from the temple services the sick, the infirm, the deformed, the unclean, and many other people who did not measure up to the standards set by them for temple access. It was this omission of many people from their religious activities that caused Jesus to accuse the Pharisees of teaching as doctrine the precepts of men (Mark 7:6–9). The passage continues with God's plan to form the "new Israel" and to set over them one shepherd, and gather them together to a land where they will live securely; and the inference here is to a place like America. This land is certainly a renowned planting place and this nation has exported farm products to many nations of the world. This land became known as the land of the free, and descriptive phrases in our official government documents such as, "freedom and justice for all," have caused all the world to recognize and admire this nation. Considering all the descriptive phrases in the Bible about the gathering together of God's people, It is a proper conclusion that this country is the place to which they were gathered. Read a statement from a recent Sunday school lesson.

> European immigrants to America in the seventeenth and eighteenth centuries used the dream in Daniel 7 to frame their escape from oppressive governments. Immigrants sought release from religious persecution and drew on Daniel's dream to illustrate their cause. They believed that God was giving them a new land in which to build an everlasting kingdom. They claimed God's authority for the communities and churches they established in the New World.
>
> Sunday School Quarterly, First Quarter, 2013

Our founding fathers were devout Christians and sought God's guidance when forming our government. Read now the prayer offered at the First Continental Congress.

PORK, BEEF, CHICKEN AND RIBS

O Lord our Heavenly Father, high and mighty King of kings, and Lord of lords, who dost from thy throne behold all the dwellers on earth and reignest with power supreme and uncontrolled over all the Kingdoms, Empires and Governments; look down in mercy, we beseech thee, on these our American States, who have fled to thee from the rod of the oppressor and thrown themselves on thy gracious protection, desiring to be henceforth dependent only on thee. To thee have they appealed for the righteousness of their cause; to thee do they now look up for that countenance and support, which thou alone canst give. Take them, therefore, Heavenly Father, under thy nurturing care; give them wisdom in council and valor in the field; defeat the malicious designs of our cruel adversaries; convince them of the unrighteousness of their cause and if they persist in their sanguinary purposes, of own unerring justice, sounding in their hearts, constrain them to drop the weapons of war from their unnerved hands in the day of battle!

Be thou present, O God of wisdom, and direct the councils of this honorable assembly; enable them to settle things on the best and surest foundation. That the scene of blood may be speedily closed; that order, harmony and peace may be effectually restored, and truth and justice, religion and piety, prevail and flourish amongst the people. Preserve the health of their bodies and vigor of their minds; shower down on them and the millions they here represent, such temporal blessings as thou seest expedient for them in this world and crown them with everlasting glory in the world to come. All this we ask in the name and through the merits of Jesus Christ, thy Son and our Savior. Amen.

Prayer given by Rev. Jacob Duché, rector of Christ Church of Philadelphia, Pennsylvania, September 7, 1774, 9 a.m.

The gathering together of God's people, and the subsequent notoriety for the reputation of our God, was accomplished on this earth with the mass migration of people to America. This gathering together is well described in Isaiah with good indications that the gathering together being described is earth-based. The final gathering together will be totally accomplished at the end-times and is told about by Jesus at Luke 13:29. That final gathering is spiritual and cannot satisfy an earth-based gathering where God gains recognition for accomplishing it. The reinstitution of the nation of Israel after World War II does not satisfy the prophesy of the gathering together of God's people because the people referenced are Christians. Only the gathering to America of the Christian people of God is sufficient to fulfill the prophesy.

WHERE DO WE GO FROM HERE

Now, that it is common knowledge that the God of the Koran is not our God of the Bible, and his teachings oppose Christianity, what should our course of action be to overcome this formidable opponent? First, I want to remind you that we are God's favorite people and precious in his sight. He has made us promises that we will not be put to shame or humiliated to all eternity (Is. 45:17 NASB); and that those who are angry at the Lord will be put to shame (Is. 45:24 NASB). It becomes apparent in the biblical prophesies following the ransom that Christians, the new Israel, those who come to be family of God by way of the new covenant, will be a favored people and live in a secure land where freedom and justice prevails. That land is America. On the other hand, the view of biblical prophesies for the Islamic nations are bleak.

What does the Bible teach about relationships with your enemies? What must we do now? What is our best course of action? Here is what Jesus tells us to do.

> But I say to you who hear, love your enemies, do good to those who hate you, bless those who curse you, pray for those who mistreat you. "Whoever hits you on the cheek, offer him the other also; and whoever takes away your

coat, do not withhold your shirt from him either. "Give to everyone who asks of you, and whoever takes away what is yours, do not demand it back. "Treat others the same way you want them to treat you. "If you love those who love you, what credit is that to you? For even sinners love those who love them. "If you do good to those who do good to you, what credit is that to you? For even sinners do the same. "If you lend to those from whom you expect to receive, what credit is that to you? Even sinners lend to sinners in order to receive back the same amount. "But love your enemies, and do good, and lend, expecting nothing in return; and your reward will be great, and you will be sons of the Most High; for he himself is kind to ungrateful and evil men. "Be merciful, just as your Father is merciful. "Do not judge, and you will not be judged; and do not condemn, and you will not be condemned; pardon, and you will be pardoned. "Give, and it will be given to you. They will pour into your lap a good measure—pressed down, shaken together, and running over. For by your standard of measure it will be measured to you in return.

Luke 6:27–38 (NASB)

The Bible teaches to never pay back evil for evil to anyone and to respect what is right in the sight of all men. Do not be overcome by evil but overcome evil with good. It is best never to take your own revenge but to leave that to God. "Vengeance is mine, I will repay," said the Lord.

Consider what can be done to improve the understanding of God's fundamental nature within our religion and with people of other religions. In many of our denominations today there seems to be more ritual than substance in the sanctuary worship. We should always remember that Jesus Christ came into the world to save sinners and make that teaching foremost in our messages from the pulpit. Interpretation of the Bible should consider the divine inspiration that formed it. The Higher Criticism theory of literary interpretation should not be used for interpreting inspired scripture from the Bible. Our seminaries need to develop a more inclusive knowledge of the spiritual world as it is revealed to us in the Bible and should teach that it exist. Look to Paul's teaching that this world is temporary but the spiritual world will last forever. Paul also gives us wisdom which will assist us to show others and especially our Muslim brothers the truth of the gospel of Jesus Christ.

> But refuse foolish and ignorant speculations, knowing that they produce quarrels. The Lord's bond-servant must not be quarrelsome, but be kind to all, able to teach, patient when wronged, with gentleness correcting those who are in opposition, if perhaps God may grant them repentance leading to the knowledge of the truth, and they may come to their senses and escape from the snare of the devil, having been held captive by him to do his will.
>
> 2 Tim. 2:23–26

To be nice to your enemies may be good for an individual on a personal level, but how should our government act? The main responsibility of our government is to keep us safe and free from harm. In order to do this, the government cannot turn the other cheek, so to speak, as an individual might do; the government must be proactive in intelligence to interrupt the enemies' activity. Our government must maintain a strong military force adequate to deter invasion by the enemy forces; however, our policy should be to resist aggressive action when possible. We should have a fair immigration policy that provides for being a safe haven for converts seeking asylum. Our foreign policy should be to help all people including enemy nations with food aid. Our agricultural capacity is such that this country can produce enough food for another population as large as our own, and this capacity should be utilized to influence a favorable outcome in our dealings with other nations.

Religious freedom is a right in our nation and should never be compromised; however, the government must protect us from evil activities with whatever forms of intelligence is available. We have heard many objections to racial profiling and recognize the problem for the group being profiled; but this tactic must be available to law enforcement for deception is a basic teaching of Islam. The people of Islam are brainwashed into believing that which is false, that is the deluding influence prophesied by the Apostle Paul in Second Thessalonians. There is knowledge of cult behavior and treatment for correcting or resetting the mind of a person who exits a cult. This knowledge should be taught in our seminaries and schools teaching law enforcement or social studies.

We need to be especially gentle with our Muslim friends because much of their world is in an uproar because of dissension within their religion regarding the atrocities of the more militant sects and complicated by the dissatisfaction among the youth who see a new and different lifestyle from knowledge gained on the Internet. It appears that the time of confusion told about in the book of Micah may have begun.

> The best of them is like a briar, the most upright like a thorn hedge.
> The day when you post your watchmen, your punishment will come.
> Then their confusion will occur. Do not trust in a neighbor;
> Do not have confidence in a friend. From her who lies in your bosom guard your lips. For son treats father contemptuously,
> Daughter rises up against her mother, Daughter-in-law against her mother-in-law;
> A man's enemies are the men of his own household.
>
> Micah 7:4–6

PORK, BEEF, CHICKEN AND RIBS

Jesus made a statement that seems to address this time of confusion and it was reported in the New Testament by both Matthew and Luke.

> "Do not think that I came to bring peace on the earth; I did not come to bring peace, but a sword. "For I came to set a man against his father, and a daughter against her mother, and a daughter-in-law against her mother-in-law; and a man's enemies will be the members of his household.
>
> Matthew 10:34-36 (NASB)

> "Do you suppose that I came to grant peace on earth? I tell you, no, but rather division; for from now on five members in one household will be divided, three against two and two against three. "They will be divided, father against son and son against father, mother against daughter and daughter against mother, mother-in-law against daughter-in-law and daughter-in-law against mother-in-law."
>
> Luke 51-53 (NASB)

Deception is a tactic that is used effectively in war and boxing, but the Muslim practice of Takiyya (deception) has no place in negotiations between people or governments. For effective negotiations, truth must prevail. In the Muslim belief the word "truth" is perverted, for it means what is written in the Koran. The word "peace" to the Muslim means absence of conflict; but to attain it, there must be an elimination of all infidels. The practice of Takiyya stems from the Koranic teaching that when a person feels threatened to reveal his or her belief in Islam, he or she may deny their religion with impunity as long as his or her heart is committed to Islam. Sura16:108 (Koran)

There is a man that has the reputation of never doing what he promises. The people in his community know his shortcoming, but the strangers are sometimes disappointed by him after believing a promise that he failed to fulfill. Since there is never a way to determine if a Muslim is practicing Takiyya, it is likely that negotiations with him or her will be disappointing. So complete transactions with him or her at the first encounter.

Oppose Sharia law anywhere it exists. Women are discriminated against in legal proceeding and treated as though they have no ability to make their own decisions. The property laws under Sharia are skewed to disenfranchise women, and there are many examples of widows losing ownership of community property to their husband's family. Women's organizations all over the world are aware of this inequitable legal system and are actively working to correct it.

Support monogamy and oppose polygamy wherever possible. God established marriage as being between one woman and one man, and hates adultery. Our common law is based on this principle. We should brag about our gender equality and our system of recorded vital statistics, which supports the legal marriage relationships. Polygamy is an affront to God. It is said that God loved Jacob but hated Esau (the two sons of Abraham). The only sinful act that Esau made, mentioned in the Bible, is the taking of two wives. It is also said that these two women were "grief of mind" to his parents Isaac and Rebekah.

The word "apostasy" used here in the NASB, was interpreted as "a falling away," in the King James Version and probably other versions of the Bible as well. This new rendering is more exact and means a renunciation of a major religion, and Paul was speaking about an apostasy or a renunciation of the Christian faith.

Surely the Christians of the world can do something to soften the impact of the enlightenment in the lives of our Muslim neighbors; for there are a multitude of fathers similar to Mahmod that find themselves on the precipice. Logic should tell the Muslims that the proofs of the accuracy of the Bible are irrefutable. The proofs are substantial and convincing to the rest of the world, so why continue to proclaim the Bible as false. Logic tells me that a God, who insists that he does not change, will not profess one thing for three thousand years, and then reverse his position expressly for a part of the world. Logic also tells me that the teachings of the true God will withstand scrutiny from any source.

The mutilation of a human body is despicable to all people, including the followers of Islam. The ungodly and inhuman treatment of women is being rejected all over the world, and Muslim nations are not immune from the hatred of women who disagree with that Islamic teaching. In national politics the lies emanating from the practice of Takiyya (deception) have resulted in a situation where no one believes anything proposed by Islamists; and after years of Yasser Arafat with his deceptive practices, the world is justified in this attitude. It is time now for all people of the world to reject these ungodly teachings. From the teachings of Paul, we now know that the god of the Koran is the antichrist of the Bible; therefore, we have two inspired books emanating from the spiritual world: the Bible coming from God the Almighty, the Creator, the God of Heaven, and the Koran coming from Satan, God of the world, the antichrist.

The famine for the word of God ended with the start of the Reformation. The printing press, which brought about inexpensive duplication of documents and religious writings, were popular. The time of the exclusive rights to the Middle East by Satan turned over to him in the ransom agreement apparently ended near the same time. The world of Islam is in turmoil today because the new information revolution brought about by the Internet has given the young people in the Islamic nations the knowledge that there is a better way in the world than they have available to them; and they want something better. The young people want the freedom to choose how they will live. As the people gain the knowledge that they have been duped into a cult that offers them no benefit, they will reject the teachings of the Koran, and begin to recognize the truth. There is no good thing forecast for those people who reject the true God, Yhwy, the God of the Bible.

What can be said to the Muslim? You will never again have the freedom to go your way unknowing the Word of the true God. The famine for the Word of God that existed during the time of your exploitation will never again exist. You were sacrificed so that God's people formed by God's new covenant with the world could be protected from the evils which have rested on your shoulders. Now look upon the Christian nations the world over; and remove the blinders from your eyes, and observe freedom and justice. Know that the true God loves these things, and he has prepared a place for you also. Your daughters will abandon you, and your wives, and even your sons will follow; and you can no longer masquerade freely upon the earth as holy. Look back to the prophet Daniel, and see the handwriting upon your walls.

> I kept looking, and that horn was waging war with the saints and overpowering them until the Ancient of Days came and judgment was passed in favor of the saints of the Highest one, and the time arrived when the saints took possession of the kingdom. "Thus he said: 'The fourth beast will be a fourth kingdom on the earth, which will be different from all the other kingdoms and will devour the whole earth and tread it down and crush it. As for the ten horns, out of this kingdom ten kings will arise, and another will arise after them, and he will be different from the previous ones and will subdue three kings. He will speak out against the Most High and wear down the saints of the Highest One, and he will intend to make alterations in times and in law; and they will be given into his hand for a time, times, and half a time. But the court will sit for judgment, and his dominion will be taken away, annihilated and destroyed forever. Then the sovereignty,

PORK, BEEF, CHICKEN AND RIBS

> the dominion and the greatness of all the kingdoms under the whole heaven will be given to the people of the saints of the Highest One; His kingdom will be an everlasting kingdom and all the dominions will serve and obey Him.' "At this point the revelation ended. As for me, Daniel, my thoughts were greatly alarming me and my face grew pale, but I kept the matter to myself.
>
> Daniel 7:21–28 (NASB)

For the benefit of anyone reading this with a mindset that is Muslim, I will define the terms as they are intended. The Highest One is the Almighty God, the God of the Hebrew people and not the God of the Koran. The fourth beast is Islam which was formed by Satan to oppose Christianity. Now read about Satan being thrown down from heaven to the earth, when Jesus died on the cross. Remember now that this is true scripture from the most accurate translation of the Christian Bible.

> And there was war in heaven, Michael and his angels waging war with the dragon. The dragon and his angels waged war, and they were not strong enough, and there was no longer a place found for them in heaven. And the great dragon was thrown down, the serpent of old who is called the devil and Satan, who deceives the whole world; he was thrown down to the earth, and his angels were thrown down with him. Then I heard a loud voice in heaven, saying, "Now the salvation, and the power, and the kingdom of our God and the authority of His Christ have come, for the accuser of our brethren has been thrown down, he who accuses them before our God day and night. And they overcame him because of the blood of the lamb and because of the word of their testimony, and they did not love their life even when faced with death. For this reason, rejoice, O heavens and you who dwell in them. Woe to the earth and the sea, because the devil has come down to you, having great wrath, knowing that he

has only a short time." And when the dragon saw that he was thrown down to the earth, he persecuted the woman who gave birth to the male child. But the two wings of the great eagle were given to the woman, so that she could fly into the wilderness to her place, where she was nourished for a time and times and half a time, from the presence of the serpent. And the serpent poured water like a river out of his mouth after the woman, so that he might cause her to be swept away with the flood. But the earth helped the woman, and the earth opened its mouth and drank up the river which the dragon poured out of his mouth. So the dragon was enraged with the woman, and went off to make war with the rest of her children, who keep the commandments of God and hold to the testimony of Jesus.

Revelation 12:7–17 (NASB)

This enraged dragon went off to perform his evil deeds in that area of the world where God had allowed him to control by virtue of the ransom agreement told about by the prophet Isaiah. Who was given authority by the dragon? His earthly name was Muhammad. The authority to act and the power to overcome the saints was limited by the ransom agreement which expired about four hundred years ago; that agreement which was sealed about 700 BC, long before there was knowledge of the western hemisphere which became the home of the people of God, the new Israel.

> They worshipped the dragon because he gave his authority to the beast; and they worshipped the beast, saying, "Who is like the beast, and who is able to wage war with him?" There was given to him a mouth speaking arrogant words and blasphemies, and authority to act for forty-two months was given to him. And he opened his mouth in blasphemies against God, to blaspheme his name and

his tabernacle; that is, those who dwell in heaven. It was also given to him to make war with the saints and to overcome them, and authority over every tribe and people and tongue and nation was given to him. All who dwell on the earth will worship him, everyone whose name has not been written from the foundation of the world in the book of life of the Lamb who has been slain. If anyone has an ear, let him hear. If anyone is destined for captivity, to captivity he goes; if anyone kills with the sword, with the sword he must be killed. Here is the perseverance and the faith of the saints.

Revelation 13:4–10 (NASB)

The time of authority of the beast has expired. Now is the time for all people to look back on their lives and be reconciled in their own minds that their names are in that book. God has provided a way for all people to become his family and to be recorded in the book of life. Believe God.